THE
NEW TESTAMENT
DEACON

ABOUT THE AUTHOR:

———◆———

Alexander Strauch resides with his wife and two teenage daughters in Littleton, Colorado, and also has two married daughters in the area. Mr. Strauch is a gifted Bible teacher and an elder in a church in Littleton, Colorado, where he has served for the past twenty-seven years. Other works by Mr. Strauch include:

Men and Women: Equal Yet Different

The New Testament Deacon: Study Guide

Biblical Eldership:
An Urgent Call to Restore Biblical Church Leadership

Study Guide to Biblical Eldership:
Twelve Lessons for Mentoring Men for Eldership

The Mentor's Guide to Biblical Eldership:
Twelve Lessons for Mentoring Men for Eldership
(co-authored with Richard Swartley)

Biblical Eldership:
Restoring the Eldership to its Rightful Place in the Church

The Hospitality Commands:
Building Loving Christian Community;
Building Bridges to Friends and Neighbors

Agape Leadership:
Lessons in Spiritual Leadership from the Life of R.C. Chapman
(co-authored with Robert Peterson)

ALEXANDER STRAUCH

THE NEW TESTAMENT DEACON

THE CHURCH'S MINISTER OF MERCY

LEWIS AND ROTH PUBLISHERS
P.O. Box 569, Littleton, Colorado 80160 U.S.A.
www.lewisandroth.org

Cover Design: Stephen T. Eames

All Scripture quotations, except those noted otherwise, are from the *New American Standard Bible*, The Lockman Foundation 1960, 1962, 1963, 1968, 1972, 1973, 1975, 1977, and are used by permission.

Library of Congress Cataloging-in-Publication Data

Strauch, Alexander, 1944-
    The New Testament deacon: the church's minister of mercy/
Alexander Strauch.
        p. cm.
    Includes bibliographical references and indexes.
    ISBN 0-936083-07-7
    1. Deacons—Biblical teaching. 2. Bible. N.T.—Criticism,
interpretation, etc. I. Title.
BS2545.D4S77 1992
262'.14'09015—dc20   92-29609
                                                    CIP

Printed in the United States of America

05 04 03 02   9

ISBN 0-936083-07-7

Contents

ACKNOWLEDGMENTS

I am grateful to many dear Christian friends for helping to make this book possible.

I especially thank those who took time out of their busy schedules to interact with me and sharpen my understanding of the texts of holy Scripture. Of those, I personally thank David Gooding, George W. Knight III, Craig Van Schooneveld, Mark Smith, Jack Fish, David MacLeod, and Darrel Bock.

In preparing this book for print, I had many willing helpers: Stephen and Amanda Sorenson, my editors; Maggie Crossett; Allegra James; Barbara Peek; and my wife, Marilyn.

Facing the Issues

When writing to Timothy and the problem-ridden congregation at Ephesus around the year A.D. 63, Paul found it necessary to give instructions about deacons. In 1 Timothy 3:8-13, he insists that deacons, like shepherds, be properly qualified and publicly examined before they serve. Since he did not want their position to be minimized by others or by themselves, Paul promises that deacons who serve well will acquire an honorable and influential standing in the local church. They will also see their faith in Christ greatly increased. He writes, "For those who have served well as deacons obtain for themselves a high standing and great confidence in the faith that is in Christ Jesus" (1 Timothy 3:13).

But who are these deacons who gain "a high standing and great confidence in the faith"? What do they do? Why are they important to the life of the local church?

Intense interest surrounds these questions today. During the last three decades, a major revival of interest in deacons has taken place. In nearly every denomination and branch of Christianity, efforts are underway to discover God's design for deacons.[1] One study on the diaconate concluded, "The church across the world is in ferment with new thinking about the diaconate as an office of ministry."[2] (The word *diaconate* denotes the office of deacon.)

We must be grateful for all that is good in these efforts and be glad to learn from them. But a serious, fundamental problem regarding the diaconate still exists: *far too little in-depth consideration is being given to the biblical texts and the biblical parameters set for deacons.* This problem is symptomatic of a much bigger problem among Christians today, which is a shameful lack of trust in God-breathed, holy Scripture. But, as we shall see, the Scripture is perfectly sufficient to answer our questions about deacons. Indeed, the only diaconate worth discovering is the one found on the pages of the inspired New Testament. No matter how limited that information may at first appear, God, in His perfect wisdom, has given us all the information we need.

If we don't adequately consider the texts of holy Scripture or limit ourselves to biblical teaching on deacons, we invariably corrupt God's design and invent a diaconate of our own imagination. Consider the following three common distortions of the New Testament diaconate.

Ruling Executives

Many Bible-believing churches (churches to which this book is primarily aimed) have made the diaconate the ruling board of the church. Richard L. Dresselhaus, writing from an Assembly of God perspective, calls the diaconate "the official board" of the church.[3] He also states,

> One of the most awesome responsibilities of the deacon board is to provide continued pastoral ministry in the church. When a pastor resigns, it becomes their responsibility to present to the congregation a nominee or nominees to fill the office of pastor."[4]

In many churches, deacons act more like corporation executives than ministering servants. In direct contradiction to the explicit teaching of the New Testament and the very meaning of the name *deacon,* which is "servant" (*diakonos*), deacons have been made the governing officials of the church.

Even more troublesome is the fact that deacons are often placed into a competitive role with the shepherds of the local church. This practice is a proven formula for prolonged church warfare. (For the sake of communicating to readers from various denominational backgrounds, I use the terms *shepherds, pastors, elders*, and *overseers* interchangeably to describe the same pastoral body. See chapter 5, pages 60-68)

9

Building and Property Managers

While some churches wrongly elevate deacons to the position of executive board members, others mistakenly reduce deacons to building managers, glorified church janitors, or sanctified groundskeepers. This view (and a similar view that turns deacons into church financial officers) seriously demeans the office of deacon and denies the local church the necessary ministry God designed the diaconate to provide for His people.

In response to this position, we must ask ourselves why God would demand that deacons meet specific moral and spiritual qualifications and undergo public examination, like the pastors of the church (1 Timothy 3:10), if all deacons do is wax floors or mow lawns. Anyone in the church, or even people outside the church, can do these types of jobs.

The Church Factotums

Southern Baptist scholar Charles W. Deweese makes the deacon the church factotum, that is, an official who operates in nearly every area of church life:

> The potential areas of deacon service are unlimited. Deacons can engage in such diverse ministries as teaching, preaching, visiting, becoming involved in social action, counseling, leading in charitable giving, organizing, administrating, carrying out the Lord's Supper, and meeting basic needs of the pastor.[5]

Such unlimited spheres of service completely blur the distinctive purpose and duties of the New Testament diaconate and can only frustrate deacons.

In their zeal for deacon renewal, many churches have gone too far, beyond the bounds of Scripture. They have placed too much authority and diverse responsibilities into the hands of deacons. In fact, some of the same mistakes that churches made in the middle of the second century are being made again: deacons are placed in various positions of authority that God has not authorized.[6] Hopefully this book will help correct the many exaggerated claims being made today about the role of deacons.

MINISTERS OF MERCY

My heartfelt burden is to help deacons get out of the boardroom or the building-maintenance mentality and into the people-serving mentality. Deacons, as the New Testament teaches and as some of the sixteenth-century reformers discovered,[7] are to be involved in a compassionate ministry of caring for the poor and needy. *The deacons' ministry, therefore, is one that no Christ-centered, New Testament church can ever afford to neglect.*

Christians today must understand the absolute necessity for and vital importance of New Testament deacons to the local church so that the needy, poor, and suffering of our churches are cared for in a thoroughly Christian manner. This is a matter dear to the heart of God.

Stressing the significance of our responsibility to the poor, the brilliant, eighteenth-century, American pastor-theologian, Jonathan Edwards (1703-1758) wrote: "I know of scarce any duty which is so much insisted on, so pressed and urged upon us, both in the Old Testament and New, as this duty of charity to the poor."[8]

So often, however, churches neglect poor and needy people. Churches spend hundreds of thousands of dollars—even millions— on buildings, draperies, pews, and stained glass windows, but can barely squeeze a thousand dollars out of their budgets to help their own needy people.

God has given deacons a wonderful ministry of service, mercy, and love to needy people. Indeed, deacons are to emulate our Lord's example of humble, loving service to needy people. Our Lord highly esteems the deacons' work, for it is essential to the life and witness of God's church. Thus we urgently need to rediscover and put into practice a New Testament diaconate. Toward this effort I will seek to explain who the New Testament deacons are and what they do. I will do this through a careful, thorough exposition of all the biblical passages that relate to deacons.

A Call to Obedience for Shepherds and Deacons

Obedience to Scripture does not come naturally, yet it is the indispensable basis of Christian living and the basis for the local church's growth, direction, correction, and revival. I recognize that most deacons will resist change, especially if they hold a position of power. So I can only pray that the Holy Spirit of God will use the Word of God, accurately and thoroughly expounded, to affect needed change in the thinking of many deacons.

This book is also aimed at showing the shepherds of the church their need for deacons and their responsibilities toward them. For in order for deacons to do their work effectively, they need the guidance and support that only the shepherds of the church can provide. Unfortunately, many churches and their leaders are uncertain about the need for deacons.[9] Some churches don't even have deacons. Yet church shepherds today desperately need the deacons to relieve them from the many practical care needs essential to shepherding a flock so that the shepherds can attend more fully to teaching, guarding, and leading the whole flock. So I hope this book will help people think more biblically about the diaconate and become more willing to change church structures that are not biblically based.

*

Because this book is a biblical examination and exposition of all New Testament texts on deacons, I have not addressed many practical issues concerning the implementation and operation of the diaconate. Instead, I have prepared a separate guide book to deal with these practical issues related to the implementation of a New Testament diaconate. You can order the guide book to *The New Testament Deacon* from Lewis and Roth Publishers or your favorite book store.

Part One

DIVIDING UP THE WORK: WORD AND DEED

"Give us this day our daily bread."

Matthew 6:11

This is pure and undefiled religion in the sight of our God and Father, to visit orphans and widows in their distress, and to keep oneself unstained by the world.

James 1:27

He has told you, O man, what is good;
And what does the Lord require of you
But to do justice, *to love kindness,*
And to walk humbly with your God?

Micah 6:8; italics added

James and Cephas and John, who were reputed to be pillars, gave to me and Barnabas the right hand of fellowship...they only asked us to remember the poor—the very thing I also was eager to do.

Galatians 2:9*b*,10

Chapter 1

The Shepherds' Priorities: Word and Prayer

> Now at this time while the disciples were increasing in number, a complaint arose on the part of the Hellenistic Jews against the native Hebrews, because their widows were being overlooked in the daily serving of food. And the twelve summoned the congregation of the disciples and said, "It is not desirable for us to neglect the word of God in order to serve tables. But select from among you, brethren, seven men of good reputation, full of the Spirit and of wisdom, whom we may put in charge of this task. But we will devote ourselves to prayer, and to the ministry of the word."
>
> **Acts 6:1-4**

In terms of church leadership, Acts 6 is one of the most significant passages in the New Testament and should be ranked alongside Paul's message to the Ephesian elders (Acts 20:17-38) for its relevance to church pastors. Church shepherds should read Acts 6 every six months, for it is packed to overflowing with rich truths and dynamic lessons about church leadership and spiritual priorities. It emphasizes the centrality of the Word of God and the need to care for the poor. It addresses issues of conflict and problem solving,

15

leadership character, finances, prayer, evangelism, love, humility, and community. It also directly addresses the subject of deacons.

In order to understand the role of the New Testament deacon, we must begin by understanding the shepherds' role in the church. In both places in Scripture where the title *deacon* appears, it is intimately associated with the shepherds of the church (see Philippians 1:1; 1 Timothy 3:8-13). Acts 6, which does not actually mention the word *deacon*, reveals why the office of deacon was created. It resulted from a two-fold need: to relieve the shepherds so that they can give priority time and attention to the Word and prayer, and to provide official, responsible care for the physical welfare of needy believers.

The apostles themselves eloquently state the need for shepherds to be relieved of the many practical care needs of the congregation (Acts 6:2,4). In Acts 6:2 the apostles state the need negatively: "It is not desirable for us to neglect the word of God in order to serve tables." Then, in Acts 6:4 the apostles state the need positively: "But we will devote ourselves to prayer, and to the ministry of the word."

Let's look carefully at these critically significant passages of Scripture. In this chapter we will expound the shepherds' priorities, for they are essential to understanding the role of the New Testament deacon.

In the following chapter we will explore the task given to the Seven, the forerunners to later deacons. We will conclude this section with a defense of Acts 6 as the origin of the New Testament diaconate.

CONFLICT OVER THE POOR

Now at this time while the disciples were increasing in number, a complaint arose on the part of the Hellenistic Jews against the native Hebrews, because their widows were being overlooked in the daily serving of food (Acts 6:1).

The apostles constituted the first official leadership body of the first Christian congregation. The Twelve, as Luke calls them, were the church's body of overseers or shepherds.

They were responsible not only for the teaching and overall pastoral oversight of the congregation, but also for the collection and distribution of the church's funds for the poor (Acts 4:32-5:11). These responsibilities soon proved to be overwhelming.

The church in Jerusalem was growing quickly. Of course this growth was good. The Spirit of God was mightily at work in Jerusalem, and many people were being converted. The church was not only growing in size, but its social character was changing. A great number of Hellenistic Jews began to enter the company of disciples. Hellenistic Jews were Greek-speaking Jews who had immigrated to Jerusalem from foreign lands and who were often culturally and ideologically broader in outlook than the Aramaic-speaking, Palestinian Jews. Because of these differences, the Hellenistic Jews naturally formed a socially distinct group. This made them somewhat suspect by the more conservative, "native Hebrews," who were native-born, Aramaic-speaking Jews.

Despite the Christians' generous display of charity, a divisive problem arose among the Hellenistic and Hebrew believers. When it came to the distribution of funds or food, Hellenistic widows were repeatedly neglected. The Hebrew Christians, who were the more dominant group, controlled the funds, so the Hellenistic Jews started to grumble against them.

Here was the congregation's first big test of brotherly love. Could these Christians solve their cultural and attitudinal differences? Would their Christian love transcend age-old cultural and social prejudices, or would pride and fear cause division, as it so often does? Would the Holy Spirit of God be grieved by their fighting? Would their Christian witness be marred? Something had to be done or the church would split apart.

THE APOSTLES TAKE ACTION

And the twelve summoned the congregation of the disciples

and said, "It is not desirable for us to neglect the word of God in order to serve tables. But select from among you, brethren, seven men of good reputation, full of the Spirit and of wisdom, whom we may put in charge of this task. But we will devote ourselves to prayer, and to the ministry of the word" (Acts 6:2-4).

Good leaders always distinguish themselves by their ability to skillfully confront troublesome issues and to be decisive. In fact, confronting problems is a major part of leadership responsibility. Fearful leaders who refuse to confront problems have demoralized many churches and organizations. Running away from problems creates worse problems. In this trying situation facing the Jerusalem church, the apostles acted decisively and skillfully. Their actions avoided a potential disaster and led to the creation of a better situation.

Summoning the congregation, the apostles first declared their frustration with the situation. They began by saying, "'It is not desirable for us to neglect the word of God in order to serve tables.'" This does not mean the apostles disliked caring for widows, nor does it imply that they thought they were too important for such work. Not at all! They had truly learned from Jesus to be merciful and compassionate. For three years they had daily observed Jesus' burning compassion for the needy. From the first days after Pentecost, the apostles gladly served the poor and the sick (Acts 4:34-37; 5:16). However, caring for poor and sick people was not the apostles' first, God-given priority. Indeed, caring for needy people could divert them from their primary responsibility of proclaiming the cross of Christ.

The apostles have no doubt about their calling. They are quite emphatic in saying, "'It is not desirable for us to neglect the word of God.'" "Desirable" is the *New American Standard Bible's* rendering of the Greek word *arestos* that often means "pleasing" (cf. Acts 12:3). However, the word *pleasing* in this context probably is better translated as "right."

The apostles feel strongly about this matter. They know it is

18

not right that they neglect preaching the Word in order to serve widows. Although caring for widows is important, the apostles know they must not allow even this honorable service to divert them from proclaiming and teaching the Word of the living God. That would be disastrous.

We all know we need food in order to live. That is why we expend so much energy to provide food for ourselves. Yet, most people don't know that they also need the Word of God in order to live. In the Old Testament, Moses told Israel, "'... [God] let you be hungry, and fed you with manna which you did not know...that He might make you understand that man does not live by bread alone, but man lives by everything that proceeds out of the mouth of the Lord'" (Deuteronomy 8:3). Our Lord also said, "'Do not work for the food which perishes, but for the food which endures to eternal life, which the Son of Man shall give to you'" (John 6:27).

People cannot truly live without God's Word. They cannot experience life as God intended it without believing the message of salvation through Jesus Christ. Nothing could be more important to the lost sons and daughters of Adam than God's message of salvation. That is why it is imperative that the shepherds of God's flock not neglect the Word.

Moreover, the local church cannot mature or be protected from its archenemy—the false teacher—without His Word, the bread of God. Therefore, it would be an incalculable loss for the apostles to neglect the preaching of God's Word. To neglect preaching the Word would destroy the church in Jersualem and deny the world the most significant message it could ever hear. The *New English Bible* expresses the apostles' concern well: "It would be a grave mistake for us to neglect the word of God in order to wait at table."

The need to teach God's Word applies to shepherds of every age. John Owen (1616-1683), the distinguished Puritan commentator, recognized the relevance of this principle:

> The same care is still incumbent on the ordinary pastors and elders of the churches, so far as the execution of [charity]

doth not interfere with their principle work and duty; *from which those who understand it aright can spare but little of their time and strength* (italics added).[1]

The shepherds of God's blood-bought church must be willing to say with the same confidence as the apostles, "It is not [right]...to neglect the teaching of the Word of God to serve tables."

A CLEAR FOCUS ON THE RIGHT PRIORITIES

After their emphatic pronouncement that it was not right to neglect the teaching of God's Word, the apostles declare to the whole church their divinely appointed priorities: "'But we will devote ourselves to prayer, and to the ministry of the word'" (Acts 6:4). Richard N. Longenecker, in *The Expositor's Bible Commentary,* says the word "devote" "connotes a steadfast and single-minded fidelity to a certain course of action."[2] The apostles were on the right track: they were to steadfastly and singlemindedly give themselves to prayer and the ministry of the Word.

I am convinced that Acts 6:4 is one of the most important verses in the New Testament for church shepherds. It enunciates the fundamental priorities of all church shepherds: prayer and the ministry of the Word. Church shepherds are so easily sidetracked. So many good things demand time and energy; there are always many people who need counsel, programs that need administering, and meetings to attend. Thus the shepherds' time for prayer, Bible study, and teaching the Word of God is slighted. A pastor of a small church told me it took him from Monday through Thursday to perform his administrative duties, which left only Friday and part of Saturday in which to prepare a message from the Word of God. My response was to encourage him to read Acts 6 and reorder his priorities.

We must remember that the true priorities of church leaders are always under attack. There will always be too much to do. "Overbusyness" is destroying the lives of many servants of God as well as many churches. Robert and Julia Banks, a leading Australian couple involved in the home church movement, write: "The cult of busyness and activism that infects Christians so much today is one of the greatest barriers to the church becoming what it should be."[3] So church shepherds must radically insist on a schedule that affirms the spiritual priorities of prayer and the ministry of God's Word. The deacons of the church, also, need to fix these priorities firmly in their minds. This is what the apostles were doing in their pronouncement to the congregation.

Prayer

Acts 6:1-4 can be called a success story because the apostles demonstrated that they had learned their lessons from Jesus. What enabled them to so confidently state their priorities? They had been with Jesus. They had seen Him live and minister as a man of prayer and the Word (Mark 1:35-39). Like their Master, they were men of prayer. Prayer had become a major part of their work. They were not building ships for the fishing industry in Galilee; they were building people for God. They were involved in spiritual conflict over the souls of men and women. Therefore, prayer was one of their foremost duties.

The shepherds of God's precious flock must understand that *prayer is the shepherds' work*, and that it requires time and energy. Hudson Taylor, founder of the China Inland Mission, once cautioned, "Do not be so busy with the work of Christ (or anything else) that you have no strength left for praying. True prayer requires strength." William Carey, father of modern missions and missionary to India, has been quoted as saying, "Prayer is my real business! Cobbling shoes is a sideline; it just helps me pay expenses." Prayer is clearly the shepherds' real business. Shepherds would do well to keep the words of James before them in all their pastoral labors: "The effective prayer of a righteous man can accomplish much" (James 5:16).

Much more should be said about the indispensable role that prayer plays in the shepherds' ministry, but space does not permit.

So I will conclude with a stirring challenge and sound counsel from Paul E. Billheimer's inspiring book, *Destined for the Throne:*

> A church without an intelligent, well-organized, and sys-
> tematic prayer program is simply operating a religious
> treadmill.... Any church program, no matter how impres-
> sive, if it is not supported by an adequate prayer program,
> is little more than an ecclesiastical treadmill. It is doing
> little or no damage to Satan's kingdom....
>
> Does anyone imagine that souls are delivered from
> Satan's bondage by means of human talent, the hypnotic
> power of human personality, the charm of human magne-
> tism, eloquence, articulateness, or the magic of Madison
> Avenue techniques? All of these gifts God may use, but
> alone they are utterly powerless to deliver even one soul
> from the captivity of sin.[4]

The Word

Alongside the shepherds' priority of prayer is the ministry of the Word—evangelism and teaching of believers. Prayer and the Word must always go together. Our Lord was a mighty man of prayer and the Word. E. M. Bounds, author of many books on prayer, warns of the spiritual weakness of prayerless preachers: "The pulpit of this day is weak in praying. The pride of learning is against the dependent humility of prayer.... Every preacher who does not make prayer a mighty factor in his own life and ministry is weak as a factor in God's work."

Throughout the New Testament, we witness the priority that Christ and His followers place on proclaiming and teaching the Word of God. In Mark 3:14, we read, "And He appointed twelve, that they might be with Him, and that He might send them out to preach." From the start of Christianity, on the day of Pentecost, we read about the principal role of teaching and proclaiming the Word. Peter preached the Word and three thousand people were converted. To a room full of eager listeners, Peter said that Christ had commanded him and his fellow apostles to preach the Word: "'And He ordered us to preach to the people, and solemnly to testify that this is the One...'" (Acts 10:42). If the apostles spent too much time caring for the welfare of widows, their primary mission of spreading the Word to unbelievers and teaching the church would have been seriously hindered. The Word of God had to go forth.

Preaching the Word is no less important to church shepherds today. Note how the late D. Martyn Lloyd-Jones, of Westminster Chapel in London, summarizes this passage:

> Now there the priorities are laid down once and for ever. This is the primary task of the Church, the primary task of the leaders of the Church, the people who are set in this position of authority; and we must not allow anything to deflect us from this, however good the cause, however great the need.[5]

Lloyd-Jones emphasizes that powerful teaching of the Word of God has ignited all the great revivals of Christianity. Likewise, all the decadent eras of Christianity resulted from the loss of Scripture's centrality in the work of God. He writes:

> Is it not clear, as you take a bird's-eye view of Church history, that the decadent periods and eras in the history of the Church have always been those periods when preaching had declined? What is it that always heralds the dawn of a Reformation or of a Revival? It is renewed preaching.... A revival of true preaching has always heralded these great movements in the history of the Church.[6]

J. I. Packer, widely known author and professor at Regent College in Canada, also believes that church renewal will be futile if it is not founded on biblical preaching: "I constantly maintain that if today's quest for renewal is not, along with its other concerns, a quest for true preaching, it will prove shallow and barren."[7]

The major distinguishing characteristic of the New Testament church is the centrality of proclaiming and teaching the

Word of God. So when shepherds neglect the Word of God, they sabotage the work of God. Therefore, the lessons of Acts 6:1-4 must be repeatedly rehearsed, as John R. W. Stott, former Rector of All Souls' Church in London and an honorary chaplain to the queen of England, so aptly states:

> The Church of every generation has to re-learn the lesson of Acts 6. There was nothing wrong with the apostles' zeal for God and his Church. They were busily engaged in a Christlike, compassionate ministry to needy widows. But it was not the ministry to which they, as apostles, had been called. Their vocation was "the ministry of the Word and prayer"; the social care of the widows was the responsibility of others.[8]

Stott goes on to encourage preachers by saying,

> If today's pastors were to take seriously the New Testament emphasis on the priority of preaching and teaching, not only would they find it extremely fulfilling themselves, but also it would undoubtedly have a very wholesome effect on the Church. Instead, tragic to relate, many are essentially administrators, whose symbols of ministry are the office rather than the study, and the telephone rather than the Bible.[9]

The apostles had their priorities straight and were determined to keep them straight. The church prospered spiritually and numerically because of their unwavering commitment.

Let us heed the words of that godly judge of Israel, Samuel, that they might be burned permanently into our hearts and minds in order to guide our spiritual priorities:

> "...far be it from me that I should sin against the Lord by ceasing to pray for you; but I will instruct you in the good and right way" (1 Samuel 12:23).

Chapter 2

Appointing Ministers of Mercy

> Now at this time while the disciples were increasing in number, a complaint arose on the part of the Hellenistic Jews against the native Hebrews, because their widows were being overlooked in the daily serving of food.
>
> **Acts 6:1**

> "But select from among you, brethren, seven men of good reputation, full of the Spirit and of wisdom, whom we may put in charge of this task."
>
> **Acts 6:3**

ACTS 2

To open the Book of Acts and read about the extraordinary love and unity among the first Christians is positively exhilarating to the soul. In Acts 2:44,45, we read:

> And all those who had believed were together, and had all things in common; and they began selling their property and possessions, and were sharing them with all, as anyone might have need.

25

This was a literal fulfillment of our Lord's teaching:

> "Do not be afraid, little flock, for your Father has chosen gladly to give you the kingdom. Sell your possessions and give to charity; make yourselves purses which do not wear out, an unfailing treasure in heaven.... For where your treasure is, there will your heart be also" (Luke 12:32-34).

ACTS 4

In Acts 4, we discover that these Christians continued their lavish display of love and care for one another. Their care for the needy became so extensive that money and goods had to be brought directly to the apostles for effective distribution. Theirs was not a Sunday-morning-only Christianity. It was what life together in the visible, Spirit-indwelt community of the risen Lord is to be like. It was the kind of self-sacrificing love that Jesus Christ expects His people to demonstrate.

> And the congregation of those who believed were of one heart and soul; and not one of them claimed that anything belonging to him was his own; but all things were common property to them.... For there was not a needy person among them, for all who were owners of land or houses would sell them and bring the proceeds of the sales, and lay them at the apostles' feet; and they would be distributed to each, as any had need (Acts 4:32,34,35).

Deeply touched by this passage, the French reformer, John Calvin (1509-1564), dramatically contrasts the attitude of these first Jewish Christians with the self-seeking behavior of many Christians in his day. (His words, we have to admit, also apply to our own day.) Calvin writes:

> Now we must have hearts that are harder than iron if

we are not moved by the reading of this narrative. In those days the believers gave abundantly of what was their own; we in our day are content not just jealously to retain what we possess, but callously to rob others.... They sold their own possessions in those days; in our day it is the lust to purchase that reigns supreme. At that time love made each man's own possessions common property for those in need; in our day such is the inhumanity of many, that they begrudge to the poor a common dwelling upon earth....[1]

What motivated these first Christians to care for one another to this extent? Calvin is right when he says, "...love made each man's own possessions common property for those in need." Jesus commanded His disciples to love one another with the same kind of self-sacrificing love He had shown them: "This is My commandment, that you love one another, just as I have loved you. Greater love has no one than this, that one lay down his life for his friends" (John 15:12,13). And He did just that. In the supreme act of love, He gave up His life for them and for us. Therefore, says the renowned Presbyterian theologian, B. B. Warfield (1851-1921), "Self-sacrificing love is thus made the essence of the Christian life."[2]

ACTS 6

In Acts 6, we again see evidence of the believers' remarkable love for one another. The continuous outpouring of love and service of the church in Jerusalem was evident on a daily basis through its efforts to feed its poor widows:

Now at this time while the disciples were increasing in number, a complaint arose on the part of the Hellenistic Jews against the native Hebrews, because their widows were being overlooked in the daily serving of food (Acts 6:1).

27

Feeding the Christian widows was an enormous job that demanded considerable time, effort, and money. This was not token giving, nor was it Christmastime or tax season. This was authentic, Spirit-filled, love-filled Christianity in action—every day of the year.

A Warning to Christians Today

This extravagant display of generosity, however, could not have existed if these Christians were worried about maintaining their standard of living or if the church at Jerusalem had spent all of its money on buildings or salaries. Nothing so effectively dulls the senses of Christians to the needs of hurting people as love for earthly possessions. D. Martyn Lloyd- Jones writes:

> These earthly treasures are so powerful that they grip the entire personality. They grip a man's heart, his mind and his will; they tend to affect his spirit, his soul and his whole being. Whatever realm of life we may be looking at, or thinking about, we shall find these things are there. Everyone is affected by them; they are a terrible danger.[3]

A Brazilian bishop and compassionate advocate of the poor confesses:

> I used to think, when I was a child, that Christ might have been exaggerating when he warned about the dangers of wealth. Today I know better. I know how very hard it is to be rich and still keep the milk of human kindness. Money has a dangerous way of putting scales on one's eyes, a dangerous way of freezing people's hands, eyes, lips and hearts.[4]

Because of the overwhelmingly magnetic power that material possessions have to turn us away from godly compassion and eternal values, our Lord gave stern warnings against the dangers of greed: "'Beware, and be on your guard against every form of

28

greed; for not even when one has an abundance does his life consist of his possessions'" (Luke 12:15). Let us heed our Lord's warning, lest our hands, eyes, lips and hearts become frozen so that we cannot share with those who suffer need.

THE MINISTERS OF WORD AND DEED

The Christians' marvelous display of love and care was threatened, however, by discriminating practices in the distribution of funds to the Hellenistic widows. Courageously, the apostles assumed full responsibility for the problem. Ultimately the injustice was their fault, since they were responsible for the pastoral oversight of the congregation. They recognized that they could no longer give the time and attention required to the task of administering the church's funds to the needy. Things could not continue as they had. The apostles were busy, and as the church increased in size and complexity, so did their work load. Moreover, their primary duties as shepherds were to be prayer and the teaching of the Word, not widows' relief. Something had to be done to relieve their expanding work load.

As a body of humble, godly pastors, they consulted with one another and their Lord about this problem. After agreeing on a proposed solution, Luke records that, "the twelve summoned the congregation of the disciples." After the congregation assembled, the apostles presented a plan for solving the problem. "'But select from among you, brethren'" they said, "'seven men of good reputation, full of the Spirit and of wisdom, whom we may put in charge of this task.'"

The apostles' plan called for the formation of a body of seven men to whom they could hand over responsibility for the widows' care. They asked the people to select the men, but because of the apostles' intimate knowledge of the demanding task, they laid down qualifications to guide the congregation in the selection process. Not just any Christian could do the job. The apostles knew that the task demanded skilled men of high moral character

29

who could be trusted to fulfill the responsibilities with integrity and ability. The wrong men could create worse problems and frustrate the apostles even more than the existing situation.

By solving the problem in this way, the apostles formed a new body of church officials. The two major categories of officials in the church at Jerusalem were the apostles and the Seven. The apostles were to devote themselves to prayer and to the proclamation of the Word. Hence, their work was primarily a verbal ministry. The newly appointed officials were to give themselves to a ministry of deeds—to provide loving service to needy brothers and sisters in Christ.

In Scripture these two broad classifications of ministry are described as "word" and "deed" (Romans 15:18; Colossians 3:17). In Acts 6, Luke defines these classifications as the "ministry of the Word" (v. 4) and the "serving of food" (v. 2). Peter defines them as speaking and serving, which is the same as word and deed. He writes, "Whoever speaks, let him speak, as it were, the utterances of God; whoever serves, let him do so as by the strength which God supplies; so that in all things God may be glorified through Jesus Christ..." (1 Peter 4:11). In both cases, speaking or serving, God is the source of power, the One who receives glory from what is done.

Some people are strong in both word and deed. For example, Scripture says that Moses and Jesus were "mighty in deed and word" (Luke 24:19; Acts 7:22). But most of us are stronger in one area than the other (although we must not neglect our weaker area of spiritual development). We must understand that the work of Jesus Christ demands both kinds of people. Both are essential to the work of God.

Those who are strong in word tend to be teachers, preachers, writers, counselors, shepherds, or students. For example, Apollos was mighty in the Word. Luke describes Apollos this way:

> ...an eloquent man, came to Ephesus, and he was mighty in the Scriptures. This man had been instructed in the way of the Lord; and being fervent in spirit, he was speaking and

teaching accurately the things concerning Jesus...for he powerfully refuted the Jews in public, demonstrating by the Scripture that Jesus was the Christ (Acts 18:24*b*,25*a*,28).

People who are strong in deeds, on the other hand, tend to be administrators, organizers, doers, helpers, supporters, builders, ministers of mercy, and givers. Stephanas and his family, Onesiphorus, Phoebe, Onesimus, and the women who contributed to our Lord's ministry were all recognized in the New Testament for their loving service to others, not their speaking ministry (1 Corinthians 16:15; 2 Timothy 1:16-18; Romans 16:1; Philemon 10-13; Luke 8:3). Of Onesiphorus, Paul writes, "...when he was in Rome, he eagerly searched for me, and found me—the Lord grant to him to find mercy from the Lord on that day—and you know very well what services [*diakoneō*] he rendered at Ephesus" (2 Timothy 1:17,18).

The Seven, as a group, were appointed to a ministry of deeds, although, at least two of them were also mighty in word. No matter which gifts or other interests the individual men had, as a group they were the church's administrators of charitable welfare. This in no way suggests, however, that only the Seven (or deacons today) had the responsibility to care for the needy.

When the apostles said, "But we will devote ourselves to prayer, and to the ministry of the word," they didn't mean they would exclusively spend their time teaching and never again help needy people. The apostles faced the problem that their charitable work was hindering them from doing the primary job of proclaiming Christ. Although their primary duties are to teach and govern, they are to be concerned for the needy, too. In Galatians 2:10, we see the apostles' concern for the poor when they ask Paul "to remember the poor." Paul, who God appointed to be a preacher, an apostle, and a teacher (1 Timothy 2:7), responded, "...the very thing I also was eager to do." (See also Acts 24:17; 2 Corinthians 8,9.)

Paul also emphasizes the importance of caring for the poor in his instruction to the Ephesian elders:

"You yourselves know that these hands ministered to my

own needs and to the men who were with me. In everything I showed you that by working hard in this manner you must help the weak and remember the words of the Lord Jesus, that He Himself said, 'It is more blessed to give than to receive'" (Acts 20:34,35, cf. Acts 11:29,30).

So it is not only the deacons' responsibility to help the needy, although they are the official church coordinators of benevolence. Every Christian—shepherd, apostle, teacher—is to be concerned about helping the needy.

UNDERSTANDING THE SEVEN'S TASK

If any organization is to maintain integrity and effectiveness, good management of funds and resources is essential.

Some Christians seem to equate disorganization with spirituality, but just the opposite is true. Disorganization and mismanagement always significantly multiplies problems and frustrate people. A newspaper reported that the Director of the General Accounting Office, Charles Bowsher, informed the Congress of the United States that 150 billion dollars or more of taxpayers' money would be wasted in 1992 by mismanagement: "Bowsher said the multibillion-dollar scandals...were likely to be followed by billions more in fraud, waste and abuse for a common reason: lousy management."[5]

Mismanagement and disorganization ruins families, businesses, governments, and churches. It is the product of the polluted soil of greed, laziness, carelessness, lovelessness, and selfishness. It is not from God. Therefore the family of God should not be mismanaged. God should receive our best effort, energy, and skill. The entire account of Acts 6 is a sterling example of good organization and loving care for the people of God.

The task the apostles gave to the Seven was specific. Its nature is partially described as "the daily serving" (Acts 6:1) and "to serve tables" (v. 2). The Greek word for *tables, trapeza,* is often used figuratively to mean food or meals (Acts 16:34). But the term *tables* is also used figuratively for finances, a money table, or a bank (Luke 19:23). For example, the *Good News Bible* translates Acts 6:2 this way: "'It is not right for us to neglect the preaching of God's word in order to handle finances.'" It also renders the end of Acts 6:1 as "daily distribution of funds." In *The New Testament in Modern English*, J. B. Phillips gives his rendering of verse 2: "'It is not right that we should have to neglect preaching the Word of God in order to look after the accounts.'"

If *tables* here means money tables, then the Seven were to distribute money for food daily to the widows and keep careful accounts of their expenditures. If not, the Seven were to administer communal meals for these widows, which of course would involve money and accounting. It is difficult to be certain, but Acts 4:34,35 suggests that we are to understand *tables* to mean money tables where money is distributed and collected.

In detail, the Seven were:

(1) to collect money and goods contributed to the needy (Acts 4:34,35,37; 5:2);

(2) to distribute the money or goods to the needy (Acts 4:35);

(3) to ensure that the church justly and fairly distributed the money; and

(4) to coordinate the church's overall charitable services to the needy.

The Seven, in other words, were the church's official ministers of mercy. Through them the church's charitable activities were effectively centralized. They represented the church's corporate response to its needy widows. As we all know, welfare activities can be easily abused by both giver and receiver. But the Seven, acting as the church's official administrators of charity, could ensure that the church's widows and other needy members would receive fair and highly efficient service.

Finally, the primary focus of the Seven's task was to assist the needy of the Christian community, not all the poor of Jerusalem (Acts 2:44,45; 4:32-37; 6:1). It was imperative that the new community of the risen Savior care for its needy. Among the Jews in Jerusalem, as the German scholar, Joachim Jeremias, reveals in his book, *Jerusalem in the Time of Jesus*, groups and individuals provided assistance for needy fellow citizens in Jerusalem.[6] In fact, some Jewish Christian widows may have been cut off from such help because of their newfound faith. So the Christians could do no less in the way of relief for their own.

The church in Jerusalem could have no credible witness to its unbelieving Jewish neighbors if it did not care for its widows.

That doesn't mean the Christians were to help no one outside their circle. Christians, as Scripture teaches, are to show mercy and love to all needy people (Luke 10:37; 1 Thessalonians 3:12). But the Seven's first duty, *as the church's official body of mercy ministers,* was to manage relief efforts for the church's suffering members.

From Luke's point of view, the gospel's advancement was intimately connected with solving the poor widows' problems. The gospel had to go forward to the ends of the earth, but at the same time needy members of the Christian community had to be supported or the gospel message would lose credibility. Immediately after Luke records the appointment of the Seven to care for poor widows, he writes, "And the word of God kept on spreading; and the number of the disciples continued to increase greatly in Jerusalem..." (Acts 6:7).

Chapter 3

Official Public Recognition

> And the statement found approval with the whole con-
> gregation; and they chose Stephen, a man full of faith and of the
> Holy Spirit, and Philip, Prochorus, Nicanor, Timon, Parmenas
> and Nicolas, a proselyte from Antioch. And these they brought
> before the apostles; and after praying, they laid their hands on
> them.
>
> **Acts 6:5,6**

THE APOSTLES SOLICIT
CONGREGATIONAL INVOLVEMENT

The conflict between the Hellenistic and Hebrew Jews in Jerusalem could have turned into an ugly church division that lasted for
decades. Instead, acting in humble accord with one another and
the congregation, the apostles peacefully resolved the highly
explosive situation. Acts 6 magnificently illustrates that the
apostles had learned (after numerous failures of fighting among
themselves for name and position) the distinctive principles of
Christlike leadership (Matthew 23:1-12; Mark 9:30-35; 10:35-45;
Luke 22:24-27). They had learned to be humble and loving
shepherds.

As a wise pastoral body, the Twelve knew the importance of

35

involving the entire congregation in solving this problem. The apostles could have acted without the whole congregation, but they didn't, for several key reasons.

First, the apostles knew that they needed to treat the congregation as brothers and sisters in Christ who were indwelt by the Holy Spirit of God. The apostles were not the people's priestly clerics, and the people were not their disciples.

Second, the apostles knew that the money belonged to the people, and the widows were the people's responsibility. So the problem was everyone's problem. The congregation had to share in the responsibility of planning and administering its charitable business.

Third, the apostles sought to protect themselves from potential, sinister charges regarding money and power. The apostles were all Hebrews, not Hellenistic Jews. According to the apostles' plan, the congregation could pick administrators who represented them more equitably. In this way, the apostles could not be accused of partiality.

This was important because, in all likelihood, even the apostles were financially supported by the congregation. If the apostles picked their own men to administer the relief efforts, people could accuse the apostles of controlling the money. The apostles, however, were not concerned about money and control. They were not greedy. Their decision to delegate the responsibility of handling the church's charitable funds to others should be an example to Christian leaders today who think they must control everything, especially the money.

The Congregation Selects Seven Men

The congregation responded to the apostles' plan with unanimous approval: "And the statement found approval with the whole congregation." The congregation immediately proceeded to choose seven men. Luke writes, "They chose Stephen, a man full of faith and of the Holy Spirit, and Philip, Prochorus, Nicanor, Timon, Parmenas and Nicolas, a proselyte from Antioch."

Exactly how the congregation in Jerusalem selected seven of its men is not recorded. It would not have been difficult for the congregation to organize itself for such a selection, for they had ample examples to follow. When feeding massive numbers of people, for instance, our Lord quickly organized them into manageable groups "of hundreds and of fifties" for orderly distribution (Mark 6:40). From its earliest days, the nation of Israel was organized into precisely defined, manageable groups for communication, war, service, and travel (Exodus 13:18; 18:13- 27; 36:6; Numbers 2:2ff; 7:2; 1 Kings 4:7). Congregational decisions and operations were conducted primarily through representatives or heads of clans and towns (Compare Leviticus 4:13 with 4:15; Exodus 3:15,16; compare Exodus 4:29 with 4:31; Exodus 19:7,8; Deuteronomy 21:1,2,6-9). So it is quite possible that the congregation in Jerusalem was already organized into similar manageable units. Such organization would enable issues to be decided and information to be passed along quickly (Acts 12:12,17; Acts 15:4,6,22; 21:17,18).

THE SEVEN RECEIVE THE APOSTLES' APPROVAL

After selecting the Seven, the congregation presented them to the apostles for official approval. Rather than immediately sending the Seven out to work, the congregation brought them to the apostles, who commissioned them in an official and public way, by the laying on of hands and prayer.[1]

It is only natural that the apostles would be responsible for placing the Seven in charge of the church's money and ministries to the needy. Indeed, the apostles' proposed plan, as outlined in verse 3, states that the apostles would "put in charge of this task" those selected by the congregation:

> "But select from among you, brethren, seven men of good reputation, full of the Spirit and of wisdom, whom *we may put in charge of this task*" (italics added).

37

The subject of the Greek verb that means "put in charge" (first person plural) is the twelve apostles. The subject of the Greek verb that means "select" (second person plural) is the "congregation of the disciples." The Greek verb that means "put in charge," *kathistēmi*, is often used to express appointment to an official position, such as the appointment of a judge or governor (Acts 7:10). It can also express appointment in an unofficial sense. Either way, the verb indicates a sense of authority, as R. J. Knowling in *The Expositor's Greek Testament* states: "The verb implies at all events an exercise of authority."[2]

The apostles could officially place the Seven in charge of helping the church's needy and distributing church finances because they had the authority, as Christ's chosen apostles, to do so (Ephesians 2:19,20). Therefore, it is best to understand that the congregation chose the seven men and the apostles officially installed them.

The Laying on of Hands

When the apostles installed the Seven, Scripture says, "they laid their hands on them" (Acts 6:6). This is the first recorded example of the laying on of hands in the Christian community. The imposition of hands is used for various reasons in the Bible, but as James Orr, a well-known Scottish apologist for orthodox Christianity at the turn of the century, writes, "The primary idea seems to be that of conveyance or transference (cf. Leviticus 16:21) but, conjoined with this, in certain instances are the ideas of identification and of devotion to God."[3]

Looking first at Old Testament examples, we note that the laying on of hands was used to:

- convey blessing (Genesis 48:14)
- identify with a sacrifice to God (Leviticus 1:4)
- transfer sin (Leviticus 16:21)
- transfer defilement (Leviticus 24:14)
- identify man's actions with God's (2 Kings 13:16)

- set people apart, such as in conveying a special commission, responsibility, or authority (Numbers 8:10,14; 27:15-23; Deuteronomy 34:9)

In the New Testament, the laying on of hands was used to:

- convey blessing (Matthew 19:15; Mark 10:16)
- convey the Holy Spirit's healing power (Mark 6:5; 8:23,25; 16:18; Luke 4:40; 13:13; Acts 9:12; 19:11; 28:8)
- convey the Holy Spirit to certain believers through the apostles' hands (Acts 8:17-19; 19:6)
- convey healing and the Holy Spirit to Paul through Ananias' hands (Acts 9:17)
- convey a spiritual gift to Timothy through Paul's hands (2 Timothy 1:6)
- set apart or place in office (Acts 6:6; 13:3; 1 Timothy 4:14; 5:22)

The New Testament contains no normative regulations for the laying on of hands. It is not a prescribed practice such as baptism or the Lord's Supper, nor is it restricted to a particular person or group in the church (Acts 9:12; 13:3). So the precise significance of the laying on of hands is difficult to determine at times. We do know that the imposition of hands, like fasting, was practiced by the first Christians because it was useful and a blessing to all. Christians are free, then, to use the laying on of hands if they desire, or to refrain from its practice if it leads to misunderstanding.

Because of confusion or superstition surrounding the laying on of hands, many churches today avoid its use entirely. That is unfortunate because the laying on of hands can be a meaningful public act.

In light of this background, it seems reasonable to assume that the imposition of hands in Acts 6 visually expressed the apostles' blessing, commissioned the Seven to a special task (Numbers 27:22,23), and transferred the authority to do the job.

Because of the Seven's responsible task of handling large sums of money (Acts 4:34-37) and the growing tensions between the Hellenistic Jews and Hebrews, the apostles knew that the situation demanded an official, public act of appointment.

The laying on of hands in Acts 6, however, did not install the Seven to higher ministerial positions (priest or minister), nor did it make the Seven successors to the apostles. It was not ordination that authorized them to preach and administer the sacraments. It did not convey grace or the Holy Spirit, for the Seven were already filled with the Holy Spirit. Rather, *the laying on of hands commissioned the Seven to serve the needy.* How different this is from customary traditions of laying hands only on the highest clergy!

THE IMPORTANCE OF THE SEVEN'S TASK

The laying on of hands, along with the early appearance of this account in Acts, indicates the significance and necessity of the Seven's task. Some people might find it hard to believe that appointing men to care for poor widows and handle money would require the laying on of the apostles' hands. Those who don't understand why the apostles took this matter so seriously don't understand how important the care of the poor is in God's eyes. As the Scripture says, "This is pure and undefiled religion in the sight of our God and Father, to visit orphans and widows in their distress..." (James 1:27*a*).

The saintly, Scottish revivalist and pastor Robert Murray McCheyne (1813-1843) understood the importance of giving to the poor and used the strongest possible words to teach his congregation in Dundee, Scotland, the necessity of giving to needy people. Prayerfully read the following closing words of his sermon on Acts 20:35, "It is more blessed to give than to receive":

I fear there are some Christians among you to whom Christ cannot say ["Well done, good and faithful servant"].

Your haughty dwelling raises amidst of thousands who have scarce a fire to warm themselves at, and have but little clothing to keep out the biting frost; and yet you never darkened their door. You heave a sigh, perhaps, at a distance; but you do not visit them. Ah! my dear friends! I am concerned for the poor, but more for you. I know not what Christ will say to you in the great day. You seem to be Christians, and yet you care not for his poor. Oh, what a change will pass upon you as you enter the gates of heaven! You will be saved, but that will be all. There will be no abundant entrance for you: 'He that soweth sparingly shall reap also sparingly'.

I fear there are many hearing me who may know well that they are not Christians, because they do not love to give. To give largely and liberally, not grudging at all, requires a new heart; an old heart would rather part with its life-blood than its money. Oh, my friends! enjoy your money; make the most of it; give none away; enjoy it quickly, for I can tell you, you will be beggars throughout eternity.[4]

John Owen reminds us that many of the first Christians were poor: "Many of them who first received it were of the state and condition, as the Scripture everywhere testifieth: 'The poor are evangelized,' Matt. 11:5; 'God hath chosen the poor,' James 2:5."[5] Therefore, care for the poor and needy, Owen adds, was "one of the most eminent graces and duties of the church in those days."[6] We must never, he cautions, treat flippantly this important responsibility to the poor and disadvantaged:

...if all churches, and all the members of them, would wisely consider how eminent is this grace, how excellent is this duty, of making provision for the poor,—how much the glory of Christ and honour of the gospel are concerned herein; for whereas, for the most part, it is looked on as an ordinary work, to be performed transiently and cursorily, scarce deserving any of the time which is allotted unto the church's public service and duties, it is indeed one of the most eminent duties of Christian societies...."[7]

Biblical commentator William Barclay relates an old legend that beautifully illustrates the value of the poor and the importance of caring for them:

> In the days of the terrible Decian persecution in Rome, the Roman authorities broke into a Christian Church. They were out to loot the treasures which they believed the Church to possess. The Roman prefect demanded from Laurentius, the deacon: "Show me your treasures at once." Laurentius pointed at the widows and orphans who were being supplied, "These," he said, "are the treasures of the Church."[8]

No wonder the Seven were commissioned for their work through the laying on of hands! Thereby they were given official status to handle the important work of caring for the church's needy. The Seven formed a distinct body of officials who were separate from the apostles. They were not equal with the apostles, nor were they junior apostles or shepherds in training. They did not become assistants to the apostles. The Seven formed a separate but complementary ministry to that of the apostles.

WHY THE NEED FOR OFFICIAL SERVANTS

First Peter 4:10 affirms that every Christian has a spiritual gift from God that is to be used in serving others: "As each one has received a special gift, employ it in serving one another, as good stewards of the manifold grace of God." If all Christians are to be servants, why then were designated, official servants needed to minister to the needy in the Jerusalem church?

Acts 6 demonstrates that certain service tasks require people who have select skills and proven moral character. Administering large amounts of charitable funds, for instance, requires people who possess irreproachable character, godly wisdom, and administrative skills. The sad truth is, some Christians steal. For these Christians it is too great a temptation to hold large amounts of money. Therefore, qualified, official servants are needed to perform these duties.

Furthermore, the Bible warns that the poor, especially widows, are vulnerable to exploitation. Jesus said to beware of the scribes "who devour widows' houses" (Luke 20:47). Likewise, religious swindlers abound, preying on widows and the elderly. No church should expose people who need the most protection and care to unknown or unstable people. So, select servants will always be needed to officially represent the local church in delicate matters of trust and to coordinate the church's charity.

A FINAL WARNING

Acts 6 is not a list of regulations and rules, so it should not be interpreted as a strict blueprint to be followed in every detail. For example, the apostles asked that seven men must be chosen. The question arises, then, if that means every church must have seven deacons. Some Christians of the second, third, and fourth centuries believed this and allowed only seven deacons per city. The council of Neo-Caesarea in the year A.D. 315 stated in one of its canons that the number of deacons in a city must be seven.

The number seven, however, met the unique needs of the church at Jerusalem, as did the other detailed procedures of the apostles' plan. Thus a local church today has flexibility in how its deacons are chosen, how many are selected, and what they specifically are to do. As long as the deacons enable the shepherds of the church to carry out their primary duties, and as long as the deacons minister to the congregation's welfare needs, they are doing their job.

Chapter 4

Acts 6:
The Prototype for
Deacons

> **Inasmuch as many have undertaken to compile an account of the things accomplished among us, just as those who from the beginning were eyewitnesses and servants of the word have handed them down to us, it seemed fitting for me as well, having investigated everything carefully from the beginning, to write it out for you in consecutive order, most excellent Theophilus; so that you might know the exact truth about the things you have been taught.**
>
> **Luke 1:1-4**

Can we legitimately assume that the Seven in Acts 6 are the forerunners to the later deacons? In the two passages in which Paul mentions deacons, Philippians 1:1 and 1 Timothy 3:8-13, he offers no explanation of the deacons' origin or of their duties. His readers, of course, already knew the deacons' origin and responsibilities. But where do Christians today find such an explanation?

Although Luke does not state that the seven men mentioned in Acts 6 were the first deacons, many commentators since the middle of the second century have assumed that the Seven were the first deacons. Irenaeus (A.D. c.130-c.200), bishop of Lyons in

Gaul (modern France), was the first writer to clearly identify the Seven as "deacons."[1]

OBJECTIONS TO THE SEVEN AS THE PROTOTYPE OF DEACONS

Other biblical commentators, however, dismiss the idea that Acts 6 has anything to do with deacons. Gordon Fee, professor of New Testament at Regent College in Vancouver, Canada, claims:

> An appeal to Acts 6:1-6 is of no value, since those men are not called deacons. In fact they are clearly ministers of the Word among Greek-speaking Jews, who eventually accrue the title "the Seven" (Acts 21:8), which distinguishes them in a way similar to "the Twelve."[2]

Although Luke does not state explicitly that the Seven were the first deacons, the content of Luke's account, in which the apostles officially appointing a body of men to administer church funds to the needy, leads many people to conclude that there is a definite connection. Surely Acts 6 should not be brushed aside. As we will see, Dr. Fee's objections, which represent the most common objections, are misleading and unsound.

The Missing Word

It is a mistake to conclude that because the Seven are not actually called *deacons*, there is no connection between the Seven mentioned in Acts and the deacons mentioned in Paul's epistles. The fact that Luke does not state that the Seven are deacons is consistent with his style of historical reporting in both the Gospel of Luke and the Acts of the Apostles.

Luke is very accurate in writing history, particularly in his use of terminology for persons and places. Concerning Luke's ability as a historian, the late F. F. Bruce, one of the most prolific and distinguished commentators of the twentieth century, quotes the distinguished historian Eduard Meyer's evaluation of Luke:

> Eduard Meyer, the greatest twentieth-century historian of classical antiquity, considered Luke the one great historian who joins the last of the genuinely Greek historians, Polybius, to the greatest of Christian historians, Eusebius. Luke's work, he reckoned, "in spite of its more restricted content, bears the same character as those of the great historians, of a Polybius, a Livy, and many others."[3]

When Luke refers to Philip in Acts 21:8, he identifies him as an evangelist and "one of the seven," but does not identify him as a deacon. The reason for this identification is that Luke accurately represents the historical situation and terminology used at the time of the events of Acts 6. Undoubtedly the office-title *deacon*, (Greek, *diakonos*, which means "servant"), was not used at that time in the church's development. Even though Luke knew that people were called deacons in his day, he did not give in to the temptation of making the history of Acts fit later church development and terminology. In other words, he did not write anachronistically. Thus "the record of Acts," Bruce states, "is true to its 'dramatic' date, i.e., to the date of the events and developments which it relates."[4]

We might think that Luke should have at least commented on the connection between the Seven and the deacons, but again that was not his method of historical writing. For example, Luke does not tell us the position that our Lord's half brother, James, held in the church, although James is a predominant figure in the Jerusalem church and was most likely an apostle (Galatians 1:19). Luke never clearly states that Paul—the great apostle to the Gentiles—was an apostle, although his apostleship is evident in Acts. (The statement in Acts 14:4 about Paul's apostleship is somewhat ambiguous.[5])

Luke records momentous events during the beginning years

of Christianity without adding any special comments (Acts 8:5-19; 10:1-48; 13:1-4). He does not match theological solutions or explanations with difficult-to-understand events or practices (Acts 8:14-17; 19:1-7,12; 21:23-26). Likewise, in Acts 6, Luke records no special name or title for this group of men.

A man eminently qualified to evaluate Luke's historical accuracy and style is Sir William Ramsay (1851-1939), who is known for his brilliant, pioneer archeological and historical research on Acts. Ramsay writes:

> It is rare to find a narrative so simple and so little forced as that of *Acts*. It is a mere uncoloured recital of the important facts in the briefest possible terms. The narrator's individuality and his personal feelings and preferences are almost wholly suppressed.... It would be difficult in the whole range of literature to find a work where there is less attempt at pointing a moral or drawing a lesson from the facts. The narrator is persuaded that the facts themselves in their barest form are a perfect lesson and a complete instruction, and he feels that it would be an impertinence and even an impiety to intrude his individual views into the narrative.[6]

Dr. David Gooding, former professor of Greek at Queen's University, Belfast, Ireland, and an expert on the Greek Old Testament, the *Septuagint*, also comments on Luke's style of historical reporting: "Luke...has added the barest minimum of interpretative comment beyond his record of the facts. He has not even invented titles for his sections."[7] Therefore, the fact that Luke does not refer to the Seven as deacons or explain the relationship of the Seven to the later deacons is not surprising. His account speaks for itself.

Missing Word, But Not Missing Concept

Although the word *diakonos*, the Greek word for *deacon,* does not appear in Acts 6, the concept of an official body of servants who lovingly serve others does appear. Furthermore, although *diakonos* does not appear, its corresponding noun, *diakonia*, and verb, *diakoneō*, do. The noun and verb are used to describe the congregation's daily work of providing material help for needy widows.

• "...their widows were being overlooked in the daily *serving* [*diakonia*] of food" (Acts 6:1*b*; italics added).

• "'It is not desirable for us to neglect the word of God in order *to serve* [*diakoneō*] tables'" (Acts 6:2*b*;italics added).

Both the noun *diakonia* and verb *diakoneō* are used in the New Testament, not only in the sense of general service but in the narrower, even technical, sense of attending to people's bodily sufferings and material needs. Such is the case in Acts 6.[8]

The word *diakonos* is plainly used three times in the New Testament to refer to the holder of a specific office (Philippians 1:1; 1 Timothy 3:8,12). It is quite likely that the official title *diakonos* corresponds to the specialized use of its related noun and verb: *diakonia* and *diakoneō*. Professor Charles E. B. Cranfield, emeritus professor of theology, University of Durham, England and author of the massive, two-volume commentary on Romans in the *International Critical Commentary* series, succinctly expresses this linguistic connection:

> We have now seen that there is in the New Testament a specialized technical use of *diakonein* and *diakonia* to denote the practical service of those who are specially needy 'in body, or estate', and that it is highly probable that the specialized technical use of *diakonos* also has the same reference.[9]

Therefore, since an office in the church called *diakonos* is concerned with the physical needs of the people (1 Timothy 3:8-13) and since an official body of men was appointed to help meet (*diakoneō*) the physical needs of the poor (Acts 6:1-6), we cannot but assume there is a connection between the two groups. The inclination to associate the church officers called "servants" (*diakonoi*) in 1 Timothy 3 with those whom the apostles appointed to "serve tables" (*diakoneō*) in Acts 6 is quite natural. At the very least, the similarities should not be ignored.

If the apostles had appointed a body of men to "oversee" the spiritual life of the church so that they could travel, and if in the epistles there was a group called "overseers," certainly we would assume that a connection existed between the two groups. In recording the story found in Acts 6, what else could Luke have thought but that people would associate the Seven with deacons? That is precisely the conclusion of many Bible students during the past two thousand years.

In a sense, we should expect the Book of Acts to help us identify the deacons described in Paul's epistles. The Book of Acts is, in the words of F. F. Bruce, "the second volume to a *History of Christian Origins*."[10] The diaconate is a distinctly Christian institution. People would want to know its origin. Furthermore, the Book of Acts is intended to provide vital background history concerning Paul's teaching and personal practices. For instance, how else would we know that Paul appointed elders in many of the churches he had established? (See Acts 14:23 and 20:17.) We wouldn't. We need to read Acts and Paul's letters together. The Bible is meant to be its best interpreter because the Holy Spirit of God divinely designed the whole of Scripture (2 Timothy 3:16,17).

The Personal Ministries of Stephen and Philip

Dr. Fee's second objection to Acts 6 having any relationship to deacons is that the Seven were "ministers of the Word among Greek-speaking Jews." In the same way, Professor Hermann Wolfgang Beyer, in his massive study on the Greek terms for *service*, writes, "It is to be noted, however, that the seven are set alongside the Twelve as representatives of the Hellenists, and that they take their place with the evangelists and apostles in disputing, preaching and baptizing. This fact shows that the origin of the diaconate is not to be found in Ac. 6.''[11]

Neither of these men can accept that such gifted men of the Word could have been deacons or prototype deacons. However, the fact that at least two of the seven (Stephen and Philip) were "ministers of the Word among Greek-speaking Jews" must not obscure *the undeniable truth that these giants of the Word became overseers of relief efforts.* That cannot be disputed, nor should it be ignored.

We must understand, however, that there is a difference between the personal gifts of Stephen and Philip—teaching, evangelism, working miracles—and the special task to which they were appointed, which was administrating the church's charity for the poor. However, there is no incongruity between being a deacon and also being a competent teacher of the Word. Furthermore, we do not know of any official responsibilities that Stephen or Philip held at this time. They were not burdened with the overall pastoral oversight and teaching of the whole church as the apostles were. Only later, after Philip leaves Jerusalem, does he give his full time to preaching the Word to the lost (Acts 8:4-40). At the time of Acts 6, Philip and Stephen could, and did, serve as officers of charitable relief and at the same time teach.

The same is true in churches today. Gifted teachers with earned theological degrees may also serve as deacons. They may teach a Sunday school class or a Bible study in the church, but they do not desire to assume the full pastoral responsibilities of the church. They may hold an office related to serving tables and also teach because of their God-given gift of teaching. We must be cautious not to impose our ideas of deacons and church structure on the New Testament, for it gives us a great deal of latitude in these areas.

Another common error is to think that, because Stephen and Philip had a preaching ministry, part of a deacon's work is to preach and evangelize. Michael Green, professor at Regent College in Vancouver, Canada, writes:

It is difficult to decide whether Luke thinks of the Seven of Acts 6 as the first Christian deacons. It would be very helpful if so; for it would tell us...that their functions, besides being financial and administrative, involved preaching and disputing with the Jews, evangelism and the performance of wonders and miracles.[12]

This is not true, however. Because Philip baptized people (Acts 8) does not mean that all deacons must baptize. Philip's baptizing of new converts was related to his evangelistic efforts, which he carried out after leaving Jerusalem where he served the church's widows for a certain period of time. The Seven were not chosen by the congregation and appointed by the apostles to teach. Rather, the Seven were commissioned as an official body of servants to the specific task of providing relief to the needy. By virtue of their God-given gifts some of them also taught.

A New Organizational Structure

It is essential at this point that we not overlook the historical fact that the apostles created *a new organizational structure in Jerusalem in order to address a critical, persistent issue: care for the needy.* Prior to the writing of Acts 6, only the twelve apostles held any recognizable office of authority (Acts 1:25). But now, two distinct groups become evident. The new group, an officially authorized body, is appointed to collect and distribute the church's alms to the poor.[13]

There are enough similarities between Acts 6 and the completion of the apostolate in Acts 1 to suggest that the selection of the Seven established a new office in the church. (Read Acts 1:12-26.) In the same way the apostles are named in Acts 1:13,26, the Seven are named in Acts 6:5. Like the Twelve, the Seven have to meet specific qualifications before serving (Acts 1:21,22). Both groups have been appointed to clearly designated tasks. Finally, the laying on of the apostles' hands indicates authorization to serve in an official capacity. Therefore, this was not just volunteer work that was open to everyone in the community. It was an official position, open at that time to only seven men, for the purpose of collecting and distributing the church's money to its needy members.

Luke does not record what became of this official position in the Jerusalem church after persecution scattered many of the Hellenistic Jews (Acts 8). For that matter, Luke never again mentions the sharing of community goods, which he has done three times in the first six chapters of Acts. Such information gaps are the norm throughout the Book of Acts. However, there are no grounds to assume that the institution of the Seven soon disappeared because it was only meant to be a temporary solution to the special circumstances in Jerusalem. Although one theologian says, "Their office was unique and was not continued in the Church,"[14] the needy and the widows surely did not disappear from the church. They still required care.

A Good Model to Follow

No matter what happened to the Seven or to their position in the church at Jerusalem as a result of persecution, the apostles' act of forming an official body of servants to care for the needy was bound to have lasting influence. It was a great plan that met a common need, and people are always eager to adapt good ideas to meet their needs. Thus it is reasonable to assume that the Seven became at least a prototype of later deacons.

A little more than one hundred years ago, the Anglican scholar, F. J. A. Hort (1828-1892), one of the most influential and brilliant biblical scholars of his day, commented:

> The Seven at Jerusalem would of course be well known to St Paul and to many others outside Palestine, and it would not be strange if the idea propagated itself. Indeed analogous wants might well lead to analogous institutions.[15]

As Hort says, "it would not be strange if the idea propagated itself." The problem of helping needy people was common to all the early churches, so the plan implemented by the Twelve and the church at Jerusalem would have been an appealing model for other churches to copy. It would have been most natural for other churches to duplicate what the apostles did in Jerusalem. In fact, that is precisely what churches of similar history and theology do today. They follow (sometimes slavishly, to their own detriment) the practices of their original congregation and its leaders.

By A.D. 62, the office of deacon was a recognized position with an official title in at least two churches established by Paul. As "a wise master builder" and church foundation layer (1 Corinthians 3:10), Paul is the most likely person to have propagated the Jerusalem model and given it permanent, universal status among the Gentile churches. Paul was in Jerusalem when the Seven were chosen and would have had many reasons to duplicate the Jerusalem model. He was concerned about organizational matters in the local congregation (Acts 14:23; 1 Timothy 3:1-13; 5:17-25; Titus 1:5-9). We know that he appointed a body of elders in most of the churches he planted (Acts 14:23), that he was deeply concerned about the poor (Acts 24:17; Galatians 2:10; Romans 15:25-27), and that he was concerned about certain uniform practices among the churches (1 Corinthians 4:17; 11:16). By implementing the practices of the Jerusalem church in new churches, Paul could foster a visible link between the Jerusalem and Gentile churches as well as solve common organizational problems.

To be sure, the New Testament diaconate had a beginning of significant origin. Church history reveals that the diaconate was an intrinsic part of every church throughout the Roman Empire, even during the earliest days of second-century Christianity. How do we explain its widespread, deep-rooted, and persistent nature? What better explanation is there than Acts 6 and the apostles' establishment of the Seven?

Whatever position one takes regarding the relationship between Acts 6 and the later deacons, the concept of deacons, as derived from Paul's two letters, is not altered. The office-title of deacon (*diakonos*) conveys the idea of practical care and service to others. Also, the fact that Scripture demands that deacons be morally qualified and examined before they serve (1 Timothy 3:8-13), tells us that their service would entail delicate matters of trust such as collecting and distributing the congregation's money and caring for people who have special needs.

Conspicuously absent in the deacon's list of requirements are the qualifications "able to teach" and "hospitable," which are both required of overseer-elders (1 Timothy 3:1-7). This shows that the office of deacon does not include teaching or official church leadership. Furthermore, the deacons' close association with the overseers indicates that their ministries are complementary. The overseers govern and teach; the deacons help to meet the many practical needs of needy people. Thus deacons certainly cannot go wrong in exploring this passages' rich storehouse of divine truths.

Part Two

A TWO-OFFICE CHURCH: OVERSEERS AND DEACONS

Now, dear Christians, some of you pray night and day to be branches of the true Vine; you pray to be made all over in the image of Christ. If so, you must be like him in giving. A branch bears the same kind of fruit as the tree.... An old divine says well: "What would have become of us if Christ had been as saving of his blood as some men are of their money?"

Objection 1. "My money is my own." *Answer*: Christ might have said, "My blood is my own, my life is my own"...then where should we have been?

Objection 2. "The poor are undeserving." *Answer*: Christ might have said the same thing. "They are wicked rebels against my Father's law: shall I lay down my life for these? I will give to the good angels." But no, he left the ninety-nine, and came after the lost. He gave his blood for the undeserving.

Objection 3. "The poor may abuse it." *Answer*: Christ might have said the same; yea, with far greater truth. Christ knew that thousands would trample his blood under their feet; that most would despise it...yet he gave his own blood.

Oh, my dear Christians! If you would be like Christ, give much, give often, give freely, to the vile and the poor, the thankless and the undeserving. Christ is glorious and happy, and so will you be. It is not your money I want, but your happiness. Remember his own word: "It is more blessed to give than to receive."

Robert Murray McCheyne (1813-1843)
Sermon 82

Chapter 5

Overseers
Episkopoi

> **Paul and Timothy, bond-servants of Christ Jesus, to all the saints in Christ Jesus who are in Philippi, including the overseers and deacons.**
>
> **Philippians 1:1**

The first clear mention of deacons in the New Testament is found in Philippians 1:1. When Paul wrote his letter to the Philippians, he was under arrest in Rome. The Philippians dearly loved Paul, so while he was in custody in Rome (A.D. 60-62), they sent money and their personal envoy, Epaphroditus, to communicate their love and support for him.

This letter is unique in that Paul includes greetings to both the "overseers and deacons" in the opening salutation. The most likely reason the overseers and deacons are mentioned in the opening salutation is that they had a special part in initiating and organizing the church's financial contribution to Paul. Paul, therefore, acknowledges their special part. Of course, there may have been other reasons for greeting these church officials, but this seems to be the most obvious.

OVERSEERS

IDENTIFYING THE OVERSEERS

In the New Testament, deacons are always associated with overseers, yet are subordinate to and distinct from them. If we want to understand who the New Testament deacon is and what he does, we must begin with an understanding of the overseers of the church. If we misinterpret the identity of the New Testament overseers, we will most likely distort the identity of the New Testament deacons. In fact, in many churches today deacons act as if they are church overseers, which is not a New Testament teaching. Let us now consider the identity and duties of the New Testament overseer.

The Meaning of Episkopos

In the church at Philippi, there was a group called "overseers." The word *overseers* is derived from the Greek word *episkopos*. The following chart lays out the Greek and English words found in the New Testament that refer to church overseers.

English	**Greek**
overseer (or bishop)	*episkopos* (plural *episkopoi*)

• "And from Miletus he sent to Ephesus and called to him the elders of the church.... 'Be on guard for yourselves and for all the flock, among which the Holy Spirit has made you overseers [*episkopoi*], to shepherd [pastor] the church of God'" (Acts 20:17,28a).

• "Paul and Timothy, bond-servants of Christ Jesus, to all the saints in Christ Jesus who are in Philippi, including the overseers [*episkopoi*] and deacons" (Philippians 1:1).

• "An overseer [*episkopos*], then, must be above reproach" (1 Timothy 3:2a).

• "For the overseer [*episkopos*] must be above reproach as God's steward" (Titus 1:7*a*).

English	Greek
office or function of the overseer	*episkopē*

• "It is a trustworthy statement: if any man aspires to the office of overseer [*episkopē*], it is a fine work he desires to do" (1 Timothy 3:1).

English	Greek
taking the oversight	*episkopeō*

• "Therefore, I exhort the elders among you...shepherd [pastor] the flock of God among you, exercising oversight [*episkopeō*]" (1 Peter 5:1*a*,2*a*).

In Philippians 1:1, the *New American Standard Bible* accurately translates the Greek plural, *episkopoi*, as "overseers." A number of English Bibles, such as the *King James Version*, use the English word "bishops," which is also derived from the Greek term *episkopoi*. But "bishops" conveys concepts not present in Paul's thought and creates misunderstanding for the modern English reader.

In ancient Greek society, the word *overseer* (*episkopos*) was a well-known designation of office; it was broadly used to describe any official who acted as a superintendent, manager, supervisor, guardian, controller, inspector, or ruler. "More commonly," states Hermann W. Beyer, "the *episkopoi* are local officials or the officers of societies."[1]

The Greek Old Testament (called the *Septuagint*) used *overseer* in much the same way to refer to various officials. Beyer says, "There is no closely defined office bearing the title *episkopos* in the LXX. But the term 'overseer' is freely used in many different ways."[2] Here are a few examples of Old Testament overseers: superintendents responsible for temple repair (2 Chronicles 24:12,17), army officers (Numbers 31:14), temple guardians (2 Kings 11:18), leaders supervising the people (Nehemiah 11:9), and tabernacle overseers (Numbers 4:16).

The first Gentile Christians and their leaders utilized the common Greek title of *overseer* to describe their community leaders. In the Greek New Testament, this word appears four times to describe local church officials (see charts on pp. 58-59), and once to describe Christ Himself (1 Peter 2:25). Thus the word "overseers" (also "deacons") is used here as an official title for church officers.[3]

The first Christians chose this common title for their leaders because it fit well with the spirit and nature of their community. There were no sacred, clerical, or hierarchical connotations connected with the word *overseer*. Likewise, we must understand that the terminology we use to describe our leaders must harmonize with our biblical and theological beliefs regarding the nature of the local church. Titles like priest, lord, ruler, king, and father are unsuitable to describe the officers (leaders) of a Christian congregation.

As the word itself indicates, church overseers are responsible for the overall supervision, protection, management, and care of people within the local congregation.

But can we be more specific about who these overseers are and what they do? Yes we can! It is abundantly clear from the rest of the New Testament that the persons referred to as *overseers* are the same persons called *elders*. There wasn't a group of overseers and another group of elders.[4]

Overseers and Elders

Paul mentions only two distinct groups of officials in his salutation to the Philippians: "overseers and deacons." Fifty years after Paul wrote this letter, Polycarp (A.D. c.70-155), who was a disciple of John the apostle, wrote a significant letter to the church at Philippi in which he referred to the church officers. It is immensely relevant that in his letter to the Philippians, Polycarp *refers to only two distinct officers: elders and deacons.* He writes, "Wherefore it is right to abstain from all these things, submitting yourselves to the presbyters [elders] and deacons as to God and Christ."[5]

So in Paul's day and during the next fifty years, there were only two recognized groups of officials in the church at Philippi— overseers (who are elders) and deacons. It is also evident that both groups consisted of a plurality of officers.[6] It is certain, then, that the terms *overseer* and *elder* are used interchangeably to refer to the same group of men. The following Scriptures confirm that in the New Testament the overseers and elders are the same body of men:

> **Acts 20:17,28.** Luke writes that Paul sent for the elders of the church at Ephesus. But in the sermon to the same elders, Paul says that the Holy Spirit made them—the elders—"overseers." This plainly indicates that elders and overseers represent the same group of leaders.

> **Titus 1:5-7.** In verse 5, Paul mentions his previous directive that Titus appoint elders in every city. In verse 6, Paul begins to list the elders' qualifications and, as he continues the list, interjects the word "overseer" in verse 7. Since there is no clear indication that Paul has changed subjects, "overseer" is another term for elder.

> **1 Peter 5:1,2.** Peter exhorts elders to oversee the church. Since elders oversee the local church, they are also overseers.

> **1 Timothy 3:1-13; 5:17-25.** In 1 Timothy 5:17, Paul speaks of the leading role and great value of "elders who

rule well...especially those who work hard at preaching and teaching." But in 1 Timothy 3:1-13, he lists the qualifications of overseers and deacons, making no mention of elders. All the questions are resolved when we understand that the word "overseer" in 3:1 is a generic, singular form for overseers, and that "overseers" is used interchangeably for elders. Thus, 1 Timothy 3 and 5 refer to only two groups of men—elders and deacons.

Unfortunately, the terms *elders* and *overseers,* which occur interchangeably in the New Testament, came, among many early second century churches, to refer to two completely separate officials: the overseer (or bishop) and the council of elders.[7] Jerome (A.D. 345-419), one of the greatest students of the original biblical languages (Greek and Hebrew) in the early centuries of Christianity, boldly asserted that bishops and elders were originally the same:

> A presbyter and a bishop are the same...the churches were governed by a joint council of the presbyters.... If it be supposed that it is merely our opinion and without scriptural support that bishop and presbyter are one...examine again the words the apostles addressed to the Philippians.... Now Philippi is but one city in Macedonia, and certainly in one city there could not have been numerous bishops. It is simply that at that time the same persons were called either bishops or presbyters.[8]

Jerome was not the only ancient biblical commentator to affirm that elders and bishops were originally the same. Anglican bishop, J. B. Lightfoot, an outstanding biblical and patristic scholar of the last century in Britain, writes:

> But, though more full than other writers, [Jerome] is hardly more explicit. Of his predecessors the Ambrosian Hilary had discerned the same truth. Of his comtemporaries and

successors, Chrysostom, Pelagius, Theodore of Mopsuestia, Theodoret, all acknowledge it. Thus in every one of the extant commentaries on the epistles containing the crucial passages, whether Greek or Latin, before the close of the fifth century, this identity is affirmed. In the succeeding ages bishops and popes accept the verdict of St Jerome without question. Even late in the medieval period, and at the era of the reformation, the justice of his criticism or the sanction of his name carries the general suffrages of theologians.[9]

We conclude with Lightfoot's classic evaluation:

> It is a fact now generally recognized by theologians of all shades of opinion, that in the language of the New Testament the same officer in the Church is called indifferently "bishop" (*episkopos*) and "elder" or "presbyter" (*presbyteros*).[10]

Although both terms apply to the same body of men, *elder* reflects the Jewish heritage that stresses dignity, maturity, honor, and wisdom, while *overseer* reflects a Greek-speaking origin that stresses the work of oversight.

THE ROLE OF THE OVERSEERS

The New Testament speaks loudly and distinctly on the identity and duties of church elders. In fact, the New Testament offers more instruction regarding elders than on such important church subjects as the Lord's Supper, baptism, and spiritual gifts. Since the pastoral care of the local church is of the utmost importance to God, He has plainly stated His will on this matter.

Under the direction of the Holy Spirit of God, Paul and Peter charged the elders to shepherd and oversee the local church (Acts 20:17,28; 1 Peter 5:1,2). To no other group or single person do these two giant apostles give the mandate to shepherd and oversee the local church. Thus it is the biblically mandated duty of the overseer-elders to (1) protect the church, (2) teach the church, and (3) lead the church.

Protecting the Church

The Spirit of God commands the elders to protect the church from the inevitable onslaught of false teachers:

• "And from Miletus he sent to Ephesus and called to him the elders of the church.... 'Be on guard for yourselves and for all the flock, among which the Holy Spirit has made you overseers, to shepherd the church of God which He purchased with His own blood. I know that after my departure savage wolves will come in among you, not sparing the flock'" (Acts 20:17,28,29).

• "And the apostles and the elders came together to look into this [doctrinal] matter" (Acts 15:6ff.).

Teaching the Church

The Spirit of God emphatically insists that all overseer-elders be able to teach the Word and that each local church financially support those elders who especially labor in preaching and teaching.

• "Let the elders who rule well be considered worthy of double honor, especially *those who work hard at preaching and teaching*. For the Scripture says, 'You shall not muzzle the ox while he is threshing,' and 'The laborer is worthy of his wages'" (1 Timothy 5:17,18; italics added).

• "For this reason I left you in Crete, that you might set in order what remains, and appoint elders in every city as I directed you.... [An overseer-elder must hold] fast the faithful word which is in accordance with the teaching, that he may be able both to exhort in sound doctrine and to refute those who contradict" (Titus 1:5,9; also 1 Timothy 3:2).

Leading the Church

The Spirit of God charges the elders to lead, govern, and care for the local church.

• "Therefore, I exhort the elders among you...shepherd [pastor] the flock of God among you, exercising oversight" (1 Peter 5:1*a*,2*a*).

• "Let the elders who rule [lead, direct] well be considered worthy of double honor" (1 Timothy 5:17*a*; see also 1 Thessalonians 5:12,13).

• "...If a man [overseer-elder candidate] does not know how to manage his own household, how will he take care of the church of God?" (1 Timothy 3:5).

• "And this they did, sending it [money] in charge of Barnabas and Saul to the elders" (Acts 11:30).

• "Do not neglect the spiritual gift within you, which was bestowed upon you through prophetic utterance with the laying on of hands by the presbytery" (1 Timothy 4:14).

• "Is anyone among you sick? Let him call for the elders of the church, and let them pray over him, anointing him with oil in the name of the Lord" (James 5:14).

• "For the overseer [elder] must be above reproach as God's steward [household manager]..." (Titus 1:7*a*).

New Testament elders are not temporary, church board members. They do not comprise the church finance committee, nor are they a body of trustees required for legal purposes. *On the contrary, the New Testament eldership forms the pastoral body of the local church.* According to the New Testament writers Paul, Peter, and James, the overseer-elders protect the church from false teachers, exhort the saints in sound doctrine, teach, preach, pray for the sick, and judge doctrinal issues. In broad terms, they lead, oversee, shepherd, and care for the local church of God. Therefore, let no one demean their office or usurp their duties, and let no deacons think they are the church's overseer-elders.

THE TERMINOLOGY PUZZLE:
OVERSEERS, ELDERS, PASTORS, SHEPHERDS

Let's close this chapter by addressing the terminology problem that exists with the words *overseer* and *elder*. If you say, "I am a church overseer," that is a perfectly scriptural statement, but it doesn't mean much to most people today. If you say, "I am a church bishop," you will convey ideas contrary to what you intend. But if you say, "I am a pastor," people will know who you are and what you represent. To a lesser degree, the same problem exists with the word *elder* because it means different things to different groups of people.

The New Testament commands elders to pastor (which means to shepherd) the church. So, elders are to be the pastors or shepherds of the church. If the English translators had only used the English word *pastor* in Acts 20:28 and 1 Peter 5:2, rather than "feed" (as in the *King James Version*) or "shepherd," people would immediately realize that elders are to pastor the church.

• "Be on guard for yourselves and for all the flock, among which the Holy Spirit has made you [elders] overseers, to [pastor] the church of God which He purchased with His own blood" (Acts 20:28).

• "Therefore, I exhort the elders among you,...[pastor] the flock of God among you, exercising oversight..." (1 Peter 5:1,2).

To most people, however, elders are temporary, church board members who are separate from the professional, ordained pastor (or clergyman). These men, whom I call board-elders, aren't true biblical elders. They are advisors, committee men, and directors rather than working shepherds (pastors) of God's people.

An executive, businesslike board cannot and should never run a church. A true biblical eldership is not a passive, ineffective board. It's a working, qualified body of pastors that actively shepherd the church of God. Some of these elders are self-supporting; others are church-supported, especially those who diligently labor at teaching and preaching the Word. This doctrine is presented in 1 Timothy 5:17,18:

> Let the elders who rule well be considered worthy of double honor, especially those [elders] who work hard at preaching and teaching. For the Scripture says, "You shall not muzzle the ox while he is threshing," and "The laborer is worthy of his wages."

Churches don't need more men to serve on executive boards; churches need loving, hard-working, qualified, skillful overseer-elders.

In order to communicate that a church's overseer-elders serve as church pastors, which is a biblically sound position, they may need to be referred to as pastor-elders, shepherd-elders, or just pastors.[11] I use these terms interchangeably, depending on the audience to which I am speaking. Most of the time in this book I use the word *shepherd* because it does not carry all the unbiblical connotations that people usually associate with the terms *pastor* or *elder*.

I believe it is important that churches today give considerable thought to whatever terminology they choose to describe their church leaders or officers. Church leaders need to insist that the terminology used represents, as accurately as possible, the original biblical terms and concepts of a New Testament eldership. False teachers have had their greatest triumphs in redefining biblical words in a way that is contrary to their original meaning. Listen to the judicious counsel of Nigel Turner, one of the world's foremost Greek grammarians and scholars:

> The Church today is concerned about communicating with the contemporary world and especially about the need to speak in a new idiom. The language of the Church had better be the language of the NT. To proclaim the Gospel with new terminology is hazardous when much of the message and valuable overtones that are implicit in the NT might be lost forever. "Most of the distortions and dissensions that have vexed the Church," observed the late Dean of York, "where these have touched theological understanding, have arisen through the insistence of sects or sections of the Christian community upon words which are not found in the NT."[12]

Churches today must not forget that the terminology they choose must effectively communicate the original, biblical concepts in language that the contemporary audience will understand. Otherwise the church will be talking only to itself.

Chapter 6

Deacons
Diakonos

> **Paul and Timothy, bond-servants of Christ Jesus, to all the saints in Christ Jesus who are in Philippi, including the overseers and deacons.**
>
> **Philippians 1:1**

Writing from Rome to the church at Philippi in A.D. 62, Paul greets the overseers and another group of officials known as the *diakonoi* (servants). The following chart will help us sort out the different English, Greek, and Latin words that are used when the topic of deacons is discussed.

English		Greek	Latin
servant, minister, or deacon	=	*diakonos*	*minister*
serve, minister (verb)	=	*diakoneō*	*ministro*
service, ministry	=	*diakonia*	
slave	=	*doulos*	*servus*

DEACONS

As you can see, the Greek word for deacon is *diakonos*. The word *diakonos* is used in the New Testament to describe literal servants:

• "His mother said to the servants [*diakonoi*], 'Whatever He says to you, do it.... And when the headwaiter tasted the water which had become wine, and did not know where it came from (but the servants [*diakonoi*] who had drawn the water knew), the headwaiter called the bridegroom..." (John 2:5,9).

• "Then the king said to the servants [*diakonoi*], 'Bind him hand and foot, and cast him into the outer darkness'" (Matthew 22:13*a*).

However, *diakonos* is most often used in a figurative sense to refer to servants of God, Christ, Satan, the gospel, or the church. Paul uses *diakonos* most frequently, usually in reference to Christian workers—apostles, teachers, evangelists, or general helpers of the church. He refers to Apollos, Tychicus, Epaphras, Timothy, Phoebe, himself, and Christ as servants. Here are some examples:

• "For I say that Christ has become a servant [*diakonos*] to the circumcision..." (Romans 15:8*a*).

• "I commend to you our sister Phoebe, who is a servant [*diakonos*] of the church which is at Cenchrea..." (Romans 16:1).

• "What then is Apollos? And what is Paul? Servants [*diakonoi*] through whom you believed..." (1 Corinthians 3:5*a*).

• "...but in everything commending ourselves as servants [*diakonoi*] of God..." (2 Corinthians 6:4*a*).

• "But that you also may know about my circumstances, how I am doing, Tychicus, the beloved brother and faithful minister [*diakonos*] in the Lord, will make everything known to you" (Ephesians 6:21).

• "...just as you learned it from Epaphras, our beloved fellow bond-servant, who is a faithful servant [*diakonos*] of Christ on our behalf..." (Colossians 1:7).

In these passages, the word *servant* is used in the general sense of one who personally serves or helps others, the gospel, or God. It is a positive, honorable, Christian designation. In all these cases, *diakonos* should be translated "servant" or "helper," not "deacon" (or even "minister," which may be misleading).

DIAKONOS AS SERVANT OFFICER

In addition to the above uses of *diakonos*, Paul uses the term in a surprisingly different way on three occasions. In these instances, he uses *diakonos*, not in the general sense of servant, but as a fixed title, like "overseer," for a distinct body of officials (Philippians 1:1; 1 Timothy 3:8,12).

The question of whether deaconship is an office or work is easily answered: it's both. It's obviously a work to perform, yet it's an office because it requires qualifications and an examination for entry, and it entails appointment to an official, public position with prescribed duties and designated authority. Thus the diaconate is an office in the church, as is eldership.

Unlike the title *episkopos*, which is well documented in secular Greek literature and the Greek Old Testament, *diakonos* as a title for office is used rarely. Nevertheless it does occur outside the New Testament, even in religious settings.[1] The first Christians and their leaders chose the title *diakonos* for their new officials and filled the word with their own special meaning.

From the specialized use of *diakonos* as an official title for an office within the church, the qualifications listed for deacons, and the deacons' close association with the overseers, we can conclude that New Testament deacons are the local church's official ministers to its needy and suffering members. Consider the following facts:

DEACONS

(1) The term *diakonos* is used in both Philippians 1 and 1 Timothy 3 as a formal title for office, like *episkopos,* to which it is joined.

(2) The specialized use of *diakonos* as an official title corresponds with the specialized use of its related noun and verb. Both the noun *diakonia* and the verb *diakoneō* are used in the New Testament in the narrower, specific sense of practical service rendered to those who are suffering and in need.

Here are some examples of *diakonia* and *diakoneō* being used in the more technical sense of supplying the needs of the poor:

• "And in the proportion that any of the disciples had means, each of them determined to send a contribution for the *relief* [*diakonia,* poor relief] of the brethren..." (Acts 11:29; italics added).

• "And Barnabas and Saul returned from Jerusalem when they had fulfilled their mission [*diakonia*, supplying the needs of the poor], taking along with them John, who was also called Mark" (Acts 12:25).

• "...that my service [*diakonia*, charitable offering] for [the poor in] Jerusalem may prove acceptable to the saints..." (Romans 15:31*b*).

• "...begging us with much entreaty for the favor of participation in the support [*diakonia*, charitable offering] of the [poor] saints" (2 Corinthians 8:4).

• "For it is superfluous for me to write to you about this ministry [*diakonia*, poor relief] to the saints..." (2 Corinthians 9:1).

• "...because their widows were being overlooked in the daily serving [*diakonia*] of food" (Acts 6:1*c*).

• "'Then they themselves also will answer, saying, "Lord, when did we see You hungry, or thirsty, or a stranger, or naked, or sick, or in prison, and did not take care [*diakoneō*, minister relief] of You"'" (Matthew 25:44)?

• "...but now, I am going to Jerusalem serving [*diakoneō*, supplying the needs of the poor] the saints. For Macedonia and Achaia have been pleased to make a contribution for the poor among the saints in Jerusalem" (Romans 15:25,26).

Professor Cranfield most aptly expresses the significance of the parallel between the office title *diakonos* and the specialized use of its related words *diakonia* and *diakoneō*, for understanding what deacons do:

> The strongest argument—and it is a strong argument—in favour of the view that *diakonos* in these two passages [Philippians 1:1; 1 Timothy 3:8] denotes the holder of a particular office which had to do with the practical assistance of those who were in one way or another specially needy is the inherent probability that the specialized technical use of *diakonos* will have been parallel to the specialized technical use of its cognates *diakonein* and *diakonia*. What we know of the diaconate in the second century is, of course, further support.[2]

F. J. A. Hort, a leading Greek scholar of the last century, further confirms that New Testament deacons rendered practical care to the poor and needy. He says that *diakonoi* used as a title and parallel to *episkopoi* would convey to the Greek mind a position that provides practical, material assistance:

> It can hardly be doubted that the officers of the Ephesian *ecclesia* [church], who in 1 Tim. are called *diakonoi*, had for their work...chiefly, perhaps even exclusively, the help of a material kind which the poorer or more

73

helpless members of the body received from the community at large. It is difficult to account for the word, used thus absolutely, in any other way. They would share with the Elders the honour and blessing of being recognized ministers of the Ecclesia. But that would be nothing distinctive. Ministration to the bodily wants of its needy members would be distinctive, and would obviously tally with the associations most familiar to Greek ears in connection with the word (brackets added).[3]

Certainly every local church of the New Testament period would have needed to do some *diakonia* (supplying the needs of its poor and suffering), after the pattern of Acts 6. So we can assume that those who were appointed in an official sense to do *diakonia* became known as *diakonos*.

(3) The fact that deacons must meet certain requirements and be publicly examined before they serve as deacons (1 Timothy 3:10) reveals that they exercise official responsibilities of public trust. The qualifications for deacons include integrity in personal character, spiritual life, and family living (1 Timothy 3:8-13). So although all Christians should be servants and serve one another in the general sense, only a few are servant officers of the church in the specialized sense.

(4) The diaconate isn't a teaching office. It's imperative to note that the biblical requirement for overseers to be "able to teach" is not required of deacons (1 Timothy 3:2).

(5) The diaconate is not a ruling or governing office. The word *overseer* itself and the qualifications and duties prescribed of the overseer-elders demonstrate that overseers protect, teach, and lead the church. The term *diakonos* indicates an office of service,[4] not a work of rule.

(6) The diaconate is plainly the subordinate of the two

offices. Assuming the responsibilities of oversight-supervision of the local church, the overseers direct the deacons.[5]

(7) The two offices of overseers and servants, are meant to complement one another. One is the office of pastoral oversight; the other is the office of practical service to the needy.

The first Christians and their leaders established the diaconate uniquely for themselves. In contrast to the long- established elder system of government used in Israel (Exodus 3:16), it had no exact precedence in Greek society, the Jewish synagogue, or the Old Testament.

(8) The literature of the post-biblical period during the first three centuries after Christ confirm that a major responsibility of the deacons was to serve the needy members of the church. Although deacons became powerful and assisted the bishop in worship and administration, the deacons' underlying role was always to serve the church's suffering and distressed members.[6] Anglican writer, R. P. Symonds, says, "The deacon was a thoroughly well-known figure in all the churches of the first centuries, preeminently associated with the church's care of the poor and of the sick."[7]

Thus the work of the deacons, the servant-officers of the church, is to oversee people's practical, material needs. This necessitated the administration of church funds. Since the first Christians did not have buildings to maintain, the first deacons were preeminently people-helpers and administrators of the church's charity. They were ministers of mercy.

In light of the overseers' and deacons' complementary ministries of pastoral oversight and social oversight, we cannot help but think that Acts 6 is meant to further clarify the identity of the New Testament diaconate. The overseer-elders mentioned in Paul's letters and Acts correspond to the twelve apostles mentioned in Acts 6 in their position of pastoral oversight of the church, although the elders are not apostles. (The Jerusalem eldership was the only other official, pastoral oversight body in Jerusalem beside the twelve apostles. See Acts 11:30; 15:2,6,23; 21:18-25.) As the overseer-elders correspond to the twelve apostles in Acts 6, the deacons of Paul's letters correspond to the Seven in Jerusalem in their responsibility to serve needy people.

These parallels must not go unnoticed. Indeed, the principles of Acts 6 are valid for all churches. Like the church in Jerusalem—and the churches at Philippi and Ephesus—every local church needs a pastoral-oversight body to teach, protect, and lead. Every local church needs a servant body that will relieve the pastoral body and provide official, responsible care for suffering, needy members. The Spirit's instructions in 1 Timothy 3:1-13, which mandate that every properly ordered church have qualified overseer-elders and deacons, further confirmed these principles. Thus it is reasonable to assume that the early Christians, with the aid of leaders like Paul, copied what the apostles had done in Jerusalem with the Seven and named their new officers *diakonoi*.

The Difficulty of Translating Diakonos

Nearly every English Bible highlights the specialized sense of the Greek word *diakonos* by using the English term *deacon*. *Deacon,* of course, is the English spelling of *diakonos*—a transliteration, not a translation. The English and Latin Bible translators probably transliterated *diakonos* because they didn't exactly know how to render this special use of *diakonos*.

The word *deacon*, like the word *baptism*, is an English transliteration that is here to stay. It has become a recognized English term for certain church officers. For example, if you visit a home to help someone in need and you say, "I'm one of the servants of the church," people probably won't understand what you're saying. But if you say, "I am a deacon," they immediately have an idea of who you are and what you are doing.

A few scholars prefer the rendering *ministers* for *diakonoi*. That meaning would be clear to some people, but for most the term *minister* has clerical, professional connotations that contradict the concept of *diakonos*. If *ministers* is used, it needs further clarification, such as "ministers of mercy" or "ministers of service." Use of the term *ministers* does have the advantage of communicating that deacons are office holders with authority, not just general helpers.

The word *servants* is the correct English translation of *diakonoi*. However, we must keep in mind that these official servants—ministers of mercy—have been given the authority and position to administer the church's practical care ministry. They have also been examined according to certain prescribed qualifications for an office of servanthood (1 Timothy 3:8-13).

The important point is that deacons are, in actuality, to care for people's welfare. In too many churches, deacons merely sit on an executive board and make decisions. They are executives who judge how well others are serving. They are board-deacons, not servant-deacons. Let us seek God's design for a functioning, qualified Christian diaconate.

THE RELATIONSHIP BETWEEN
DEACONS AND SHEPHERDS

As most churches know, conflict between shepherds and deacons is not uncommon and can arise from both sides. Indeed, any organization with two or more groups holding official responsibilities will face tensions. The better we understand the differences between shepherds (overseer-elders) and deacons, the more able we will be to avoid conflicts. When we don't understand these differences, power struggles and misunderstandings raise their ugly heads.

The work of shepherds and deacons frequently overlaps. They must make joint decisions, pass information back and forth, and seek help from each other. For example, a shepherd might be counseling a couple with marital problems. The couple may also face severe financial troubles and cannot provide for their childrens' needs. The shepherd-elder will need to inform the deacons of the couple's financial need, but he will need to guide the deacons so that they do not interfere with his counsel. Also, for reasons he cannot disclose, the shepherd may want to limit the amount of money the deacons give to the couple. In such situations, the deacons could easily think the shepherd is acting too harshly.

These types of situations breed disagreement and ill feelings. Even Solomon would be stumped by some situations that shepherds and deacons face today! Only through effective communication, love, and trust can such conflicts be avoided.

In many churches, deacons misunderstand their role. They think that they comprise a second group of overseer-elders or that they are to provide checks and balances for the shepherds. If deacons control the finances, they often think they control the church. This should not be. It is plain from everything we have studied that deacons are subordinate to overseers. We must also understand that shepherds can perform all the functions of deacons, but deacons cannot perform all the functions of shepherds. Unlike deacons, shepherds are responsible for the overall leadership, supervision, and teaching of the congregation. This includes handling and overseeing the church's funds (Acts 11:30; 1 Peter 5:2). In the sense that shepherds oversee the entire church, they also oversee the deacons. Therefore, deacons are not independent of the leadership oversight of the shepherds.

As church leaders, the shepherds need to clarify regularly what the deacons' duties will be. Lack of clarification causes many deacon-related problems. Because the diaconate is the subordinate office, it commonly struggles with knowing if it is functioning according to what the shepherds want.

If shepherds provide poor pastoral leadership for the church, they will frustrate the deacons. Deacons are often strong and influential men who care deeply about the people's welfare. Sometimes deacons are more competent and aggressive than overseers. They get things done. They work hard. Before long, they may become critical of the shepherds, and the shepherds, in turn, may become intimidated by the deacons. In extreme cases, the shepherds' neglect in directing and encouraging the deacons may cause the diaconate to cease functioning altogether.

There are tremendous advantages to having prescribed, limited responsibilities for deacons. The shepherds' work is more diverse and general: counseling, teaching, managing, admonishing, and directing. Deacons need to understand and appreciate that their responsibilities are more limited, so they can be more focused in serving the Lord's people. We render the deacons a great disservice when we make them the church factotums.

Shepherds also need to understand that deacons have their own office and duties to perform. Shepherds who don't respect those duties, or who don't understand the deacons' role, will unnecessarily interfere with the deacons' work. That can make the deacons feel as if they are not trusted.

Therefore, good coordination between shepherds and deacons is vital to a smooth working relationship. Shepherds and deacons can implement many practical, organizational procedures to avoid conflict and misunderstanding. God expects them to use the creativity and intelligence He has given to conduct their lives effectively and orderly. As Scripture commands, "But let all things be done properly and in an orderly manner" (1 Corinthians 14:40).

Part Three

THE QUALIFICATIONS FOR DEACONS

"He who walks in a blameless way is the one who will minister to me."

Psalm 101:6b

"Furthermore, you shall select out of all the people able men who fear God, men of truth, those who hate dishonest gain; and you shall place these over them, as leaders of thousands, of hundreds, of fifties and of tens."

Exodus 18:21

"Choose wise and discerning and experienced men from your tribes, and I will appoint them as your heads."

Deuteronomy 1:13

It is a trustworthy statement: if any man aspires to the office of overseer, it is a fine work he desires to do. An overseer, then, must be above reproach....

1 Timothy 3:1,2a

...appoint elders in every city as I directed you, namely, if any man be above reproach....

Titus 1:5b,6a

Chapter 7

The Absolute Necessity for Character Qualifications for Deacons

Deacons likewise must be men of dignity, not double-tongued, or addicted to much wine or fond of sordid gain, but holding to the mystery of the faith with a clear conscience.

1 Timothy 3:8,9

I am writing these things to you, hoping to come to you before long; but in case I am delayed, I write so that you may know how one ought to conduct himself in the household of God, which is the church of the living God, the pillar and support of the truth.

1 Timothy 3:14,15

In a letter (A.D. 394) to a young presbyter named Nepotian, Jerome rebuked the churches of his day for their hypocrisy in showing more heartfelt interest in the appearance of their church buildings than in the proper selection of their church leaders:

Many build churches nowadays; their walls and pillars

83

of glowing marble, their ceilings glittering with gold, their altars studded with jewels. Yet to the choice of Christ's ministers no heed is paid.[1]

The New Testament makes the uncontested point that God's paramount concern is not with buildings or programs but with the moral and spiritual character of those who lead and care for His people. Godly leadership makes the true, spiritual difference in the local church. In fact, almost all the instruction on deacons in the New Testament relates to their qualifications.

According to the New Testament, not just anyone who wants to be a deacon can become one. Paul is emphatic about this, probably because this is where the church at Ephesus had gone wrong. Unqualified people had pushed their way into leadership positions. Indeed, placing unqualified and unfit people into the church's leadership structure is a crucial part of Satan's ongoing strategy for corrupting churches. *Thus one of the major teachings of 1 Timothy is that a properly ordered church must have morally and spiritually qualified overseers and deacons* (1 Timothy 3:1-13).

On this issue there can be no compromise without long-term, ruinous consequences to the local church. Yet, this is where many churches repeatedly fail. So God, in His perfect wisdom, has given us 1 Timothy to warn and instruct us regarding the proper character of those who would lead and care for the local church. Since this is a matter of extreme urgency to churches today, let us look briefly at the historical situation that developed in the church at Ephesus and why Paul addressed the problem of church leadership in 1 Timothy.

THE HISTORICAL SITUATION

Shortly after Paul's release from Roman imprisonment (A.D. 60-62), he and Timothy visited Ephesus. It was not a pleasant visit. False teachers held the church in a death grip of false doctrine. In order to stop these teachers from totally undermining the church's life and its glorious gospel, Paul had to take radical action. He excommunicated the two leading perpetrators, Hymenaeus and Alexander (1 Timothy 1:19,20).

For unknown reasons, Paul then had to move immediately to Macedonia, so he left Timothy behind to help the embattled church and particularly to stop the false teaching. In 1 Timothy 1:3, we read: "As I urged you upon my departure for Macedonia, remain on at Ephesus, in order that you may instruct certain men not to teach strange doctrines...."

Paul knew that Timothy faced a difficult assignment. He was keenly aware of the tough problems that young Timothy would encounter. Like deeply rooted, tough, old weeds, false teaching is hard to pull out once it has taken root. The opposition at Ephesus was fiercely argumentative (6:3-5,20). So Paul wrote to Timothy from Macedonia to remind him of his duty, to encourage him in the spiritual battle, and to formally tell him—and the church—what problems needed correction.

The church at Ephesus urgently needed reforms. False teaching had confused and disrupted church life. Christians were acting improperly toward one another. They forsook apostolic principles of church life. Senseless, unhealthy doctrines were being taught. Unqualified people seemingly had become shepherds, and good shepherd-elders were not properly cared for. Some women flaunted their riches and knowledge in church. Exclusive ideas and fighting among men adversely affected the church's prayers. Widows were selfishly forsaken by their families and forced to rely on the church for support. Sin was ignored.

A NEED FOR ORDER IN GOD'S CHURCH

As a result of these problems, Paul laid down proper principles for the social structure, or order, of the family of God. He wanted every member and group to know how to act:

I am writing these things to you, hoping to come to

you before long; but in case I am delayed, I write so that you may know *how one ought to conduct himself* in the household of God, which is the church of the living God, the pillar and support of the truth (1 Timothy 3:14,15; italics added).

In *The Modern Speech New Testament*, Richard Weymouth's paraphrase of verse 15 is worth repeating: "I now write, so that you may have rules to guide you in dealing with God's household."

One commentator summarizes verse 15 this way: "He [Paul] wishes Timothy to have before him an outline of the relation which must exist between the various parts of a congregation or household of God."[2]

The word "conduct" in verse 15 means "behavior," "one's manner of life and character," or, as one major Greek lexicon states: [to] "*live* in the sense of the practice of certain principles."[3]

The "these things" mentioned in verse 14 are probably the instructions and principles Paul gives throughout the letter. They are standards that must guide the conduct of believers. For example, certain expected rules help order a family's life. So, too, proper standards of behavior and order exist in the local church— God's extended family. Church order or proper conduct among God's family might seem unimportant to many people, but as E. F. Scott insightfully states in the *Moffatt New Testament Commentary*, Paul "insists on right order because he feels it to be necessary to true religion":

> The rules prescribed have dealt with practical arrangements, and might seem to have little relation to the higher interests of religion. Yet they must not be neglected. They involve the well-being of the Church, and it is the Church that maintains the gospel and offers it to the world. So in these verses we have the key to the inner meaning of the Pastoral Epistles. The writer is no mere ecclesiastic, more concerned with the mechanism of the Church than

with its spiritual life. He insists on right order because he feels it to be necessary to true religion. In the life of the Church, as of the individual, body and soul must work together.[4]

Paul's reasoning is simple. Since Christians of a local church make up the (1) "household of God," which is also (2) "the church of the living God" and (3) "the pillar and support of the truth," their customs and way of life before a watching world are critically important. These three vivid descriptions of the local church, writes David C. Verner, emphasize "its greatness and therefore also the importance of the way in which its members conduct their lives."[5] Therefore it is absolutely imperative that the members act in their congregational life according to Christian standards of behavior and order. In the words of J. N. D. Kelly, former principal of St. Edmund Hall, Oxford, "The gist of Paul's message is that order, in the widest sense of the term, is necessary in the Christian congregation precisely because it is God's household, his chosen instrument for proclaiming to men the saving truth of the revelation of the God-man, Jesus Christ."[6]

THE NEED FOR QUALIFIED LEADERSHIP

The principles governing the shepherds and deacons of the congregation, and above all, the moral character requirements of shepherds and deacons, are absolutely central to the proper order, discipline, and behavior of a congregation of Christian people. *I am convinced that God has given the local church the qualifications listed in 1 Timothy 3:1-12 to protect His people from unworthy and unscrupulous men, of whom there seems to be no shortage* (Titus 1:10). Some men desire positions of leadership simply to satisfy their unholy egos. Others are deceived about their own ability and character. So, Scripture wisely provides objective qualifications that test the subjective desire of all who seek to be shepherds or deacons.

Furthermore, the offices of God's church are not honorary positions bestowed on people who have attended church faithfully for many years. Nor, as we've seen, are they board positions that are filled with good friends, rich people, or successful business persons. The church offices are only for those who are biblically qualified and moved by the Holy Spirit of God to sacrificially pastor and serve God's family.

Shepherds and deacons hold positions of sacred trust. They direct and care for the family of God. They handle problems, money, and needy people. They have access to people's homes and the most intimate details of their lives. They have access to people who are most vulnerable to deception or abuse. Thus they *must be men of proven integrity.*

The leadership and service of shepherds and deacons affects the church in every way. Leaders who have good character provide better judgment, guidance, balance, and stability for the church. Those who are marred in character, however, mislead the church. Describing the essential marks of a biblical church, Francis A. Schaeffer (1912-1984) sternly warns that if we desire to be a New Testament church, we must faithfully maintain the biblical qualifications for all our shepherds and deacons:

> The church has no right to diminish these standards for the officers of the church, nor does it have any right to elevate any other as though they are then equal to these which are commanded by God himself. These and only these stand as absolute.[7]

I have repeatedly observed that the big mistake many churches make when first seeking to establish a biblical eldership and biblical diaconate is to appoint the wrong men to office. In the end, the church is saddled with the wrong leaders and perhaps suffers years of problems such as those experienced by the church at Ephesus. Insist on biblically qualified men for church office, even if such men take years to develop. Complete obedience to God's Word is always the best church policy.

CHARACTER QUALIFICATIONS FOR DEACONS

SPECIFIC QUALIFICATIONS
FOR OVERSEERS AND DEACONS

As in Philippians, Paul mentions overseers and deacons side by side in 1 Timothy. After listing the qualifications of overseer-elders (1 Timothy 3:1), Paul begins his instruction on deacons by saying, "Deacons likewise must be..." (3:8-13). The adverb "likewise" links together the teaching on deacons (3:8-13) with the previous teaching on overseers (3:1-7). It means that what Paul said about the necessity of overseers being properly qualified also applies to deacons.

To think that deacons don't need to meet qualifications for office because they are not as essential to the church as the shepherds is a big, yet common, mistake. This error demonstrates how little people understand about the importance of deacons to the local congregation. Indeed, the deacon's significance to a church is clearly displayed by the fact that their qualifications are similar to those of overseers. Compare the deacons' qualifications with those of the overseer-elders:

Deacons	*Overseers*
1. Dignity	_____
2. Not double-tongued	_____
3. Not addicted to much wine	1. Not addicted to wine
4. Not fond of sordid gain	2. Not fond of sordid gain
5. Holding to the mystery of the faith with a clear conscience	_____
6. Beyond reproach	3. Beyond reproach
7. The wife's character	_____
8. Husband of one wife	4. Husband of one wife
9. Good manager of his children and his own household	5. Manages his household well
	6. Temperate
	7. Prudent
	8. Respectable

9. Hospitable
10. Able to teach
11. Not pugnacious
12. Gentle
13. Uncontentious
14. Not a new convert
15. Has a good reputation with those outside the church
16. Not self-willed
17. Not quick-tempered
18. Lover of what is good
19. Just
20. Devout
21. Self-controlled
22. Holds fast to the faithful Word

Deacons, like overseers, have to be: (1) above reproach, (2) faithful to their wives, (3) good managers of their families, (4) not lovers of money, and (5) not addicted to wine. The deacons' additional qualifications, especially not being "double-tongued" and "holding to the mystery of the faith with a clear conscience," further reveal that deacons must have proven integrity.

The qualifications of shepherds and deacons differ, however, in that deacons don't have to be teachers of the Word. Overseer-elders must be able "to exhort in sound doctrine and to refute those who contradict" (Titus 1:9). Furthermore, the variety of character traits pertaining to the shepherds' mental and emotional stability are not required of deacons. As shepherds of the entire flock of God, overseer-elders must be mentally, emotionally, and spiritually stable in order to deal with a multitude of troublesome leadership problems and difficult people. Finally, overseers must be characterized by hospitality and must not be new converts (3:6).

Placed side by side with the church overseers, the diaconate is given permanent and universal status among churches. It is part of the social and structural ordering of God's family (1 Timothy 3:14,15).

THE NEED FOR A PLURALITY OF DEACONS

The word *deacons* appears in 1 Timothy in the plural form, as it does in Philippians 1:1. It is reasonable to assume that the diaconate modeled itself after the eldership and so, like the overseer-elders, the deacons met and worked together as a group. (The singular form of overseer in 1 Timothy 3:2 is a generic singular.[8] In Philippians 1:1, overseer is plural.)

It's extremely important to observe that, after all the problems and leadership failures in Ephesus, Paul still affirms the plurality of elders (1 Timothy 5:17,18). He doesn't order Timothy to appoint one strong leader to rule the church and deal with all the problems. From the beginning of his ministry to the end, Paul insisted on a plurality of shepherd- elders for the pastoral oversight of the churches. Thus, plurality in pastoral leadership and deaconship is a thoroughly Scriptural policy for the local church. (Timothy was Paul's personal, temporary, apostolic representative to a church in crisis. He eventually left the church and wasn't its sole pastor in the traditional sense of the word.)

Furthermore, the deacons' duties necessitated that they work as a collective body. Since they handled money and difficult people problems, especially the distribution of funds to the needy, they needed the protection in financial matters that their fellow colleagues would provide.

Not only does the diaconate need protection in the financial area, it needs the benefit of collective wisdom. Deacons have to deal with many sensitive, complex situations involving needy brothers and sisters. Several discerning people, each contributing wisdom and unique perspective to each decision, can best handle such situations. As wise King Solomon said, "Iron sharpens iron, So one man sharpens another" (Proverbs 27:17). "Prepare plans by consultation" (Proverbs 20:18*a*), and "...in abundance of counselors there is victory" (Proverbs 24:6*b*).

Moreover, a team of deacons provides mutual accountability, which deacons need in order to perform their duties promptly and responsibly. Terrible harm would have ensued, for example, if the widows mentioned in Acts 6 had been treated haphazardly. We all can become too busy, forgetful, fearful, or lazy. So we need, more than we will ever realize, fellow colleagues in ministry to whom we can be answerable for our work. Coaches know that if athletes train together, they push one another to greater achievement. When someone else is running alongside, a runner will push a little harder and go a little farther. The same is true in the Lord's work. That is one reason why the Lord sent His disciples out in twos. Left to ourselves, we do mainly what we want to do, not what we should do or what is best for others. This is especially true if we are facing tense confrontational situations with erring members. Most people will avoid unpleasant confrontation at all cost. Thus we need the loving encouragement and close accountability that a plurality (team) of leadership provides so that we accomplish our Christian duty despite our fears or busyness.

Finally, a body of deacons helps to lighten a heavy workload. Serving people's needs is the kind of work that burns people out in a hurry. But a group effort provides mutual help and encouragement for difficult labor over a period of time. Bible commentator and pastor of Tenth Presbyterian Church in Philadelphia, James M. Boice, expresses the wisdom of group effort in God's work:

> ...there is no reference anywhere in the New Testament to the appointment of only one elder or one deacon to a work. We would tend to appoint one leader, but God's wisdom is greater than our own at this point. In appointing several persons to work together, the church at God's direction provided for mutual encouragement among those who shared in the work as well as lessened the chance for pride and tyranny in office.[9]

92

Chapter 8

Five Character Qualifications for Deacons

> **Deacons likewise must be men of dignity, not double-tongued, or addicted to much wine or fond of sordid gain, but holding to the mystery of the faith with a clear conscience.**
>
> **1 Timothy 3:8,9**

> **"But select from among you, brethren, seven men of good reputation, full of the Spirit and of wisdom, whom we may put in charge of this task."**
>
> **Acts 6:3**

The apostles, both the Twelve and Paul, insist that those who serve the church in an official, servant capacity must meet certain moral and spiritual requirements (Acts 6 and 1 Timothy 3). Whenever someone is placed in a position of trust or assumes leadership responsibility in the church, the issue of proven moral character should be paramount. How, for example, could the Seven handle the church's funds and minister to its most vulnerable, needy people if they were not known to be godly, reliable men who possessed unimpeachable character?

I doubt that you would entrust your children or family

finances to an unknown person, so why should the church entrust God's needy people and resources to unknown, unproven people? Yet that is what many churches do. They are so desperate for help that newcomers become Sunday school teachers or deacons within weeks, without church officials or leaders having any real knowledge of the newcomers' spiritual or moral condition. Placed too hastily in official positions of trust, unknown and unexamined people have created irreparable damage in numerous churches.

Because a deacon has greater access to people who are hurting and weak, he can more easily exploit them. So Scripture warns us against hasty appointments: "Do not lay hands upon anyone too hastily..." (1 Timothy 5:22). After listing five character requirements for deacons, Paul says, "And let these also first be tested; then let them serve as deacons if they are beyond reproach" (1 Timothy 3:10).

The character requirements for deacons that Paul lists (verses 8,9) include:

- Men of dignity
- Not double-tongued
- Not addicted to much wine
- Not fond of sordid gain
- Holding to the mystery of the faith with a clear conscience

As we might expect, "dignity" (or "worthy of respect")—the first qualification heading Paul's list—is general in nature. After the initial qualification "worthy of respect," three prohibitions follow. These prohibitions, being "double-tongued, or addicted to much wine or fond of sordid gain," illustrate character qualities that can destroy a person's respectability. Think of the number of politicians, business people, and religious leaders who have been caught in double-talk, drinking to excess, or stealing funds. They are not worthy of respect. They are not men under control. And they are not qualified to become deacons.

We can summarize these qualifications by saying that deacons must be men of integrity and self-control who live consistent

Christian lives in full view of their fellow believers. Using the terminology the Twelve used in Acts 6 to describe the Seven, we can say that deacons must be "men of good reputation, full of the Spirit and of wisdom." That means they had to be controlled by the Holy Spirit of God—not by money, wine, or an uncontrolled tongue. Their lives had to display the works of the Holy Spirit.

Only Spirit-filled men can be sensitive to God's principles and people. They alone can exhibit Christ's compassion and love. They will not shame the church or exploit needy, vulnerable people. Likewise, we must insist that deacons also be men who are controlled by the Holy Spirit. Tragically, too many men who are doing the Lord's work are "full of self," not "full of the Spirit." Thus their concerns are with their own comforts, reputations, ideas, and advancement.

Let us now examine each of these five qualifications for deacons.

Dignity: A Man Worthy of Respect

Anglican Archbishop Richard Trench (1807-1886), in his classic work *Synonyms of the New Testament*, expresses frustration in trying to find the right English word to express the Greek word for "dignity": "The word we want is one in which the sense of gravity and dignity, and of these as inviting reverence, is combined; a word which I fear we may look for long without finding."[1] The *New International Version* gives an excellent, contemporary rendering: "men worthy of respect." The words *respectable* and *honorable* also help convey the meaning of a person whose moral and spiritual character evokes esteem from others. So, a deacon must be a man who is known and respected by the congregation. Stephen, one of the Seven who is described in Acts 6, was honorable and respected by all.

Paul's qualification, "worthy of respect," corresponds with the apostles' qualification in Acts 6:3, "of good reputation." "Of good reputation" means that the Seven had to be men who were known and well spoken of because of their good character and skills. Richard Rackham, in the *Westminster Commentaries* series, expresses this thought: "They must be of good character and that certified by the public *testimony*."[2] Furthermore, the qualification, "worthy of respect," includes the Acts 6 qualification, "full of wisdom." Men who are wise are men who are "worthy of respect." A man, therefore, cannot be a deacon if he isn't wise.

The wisdom referred to in Acts 6 means good judgment in both spiritual and practical matters (1 Corinthians 6:5). It takes a great deal of discernment to equitably distribute money and help to needy people. The problems of the poor and hurting are often complex, and there is a tendency to oversimplify matters. It is difficult to be fair and generous while at the same time practical and responsible.

As one of the first Protestants to try to recover a biblical diaconate, John Calvin had lots of experience dealing with the problems of the poor in the city of Geneva and answering their critics. Knowing firsthand that the diaconate was a difficult task that required wise men, he wrote:

> It is necessary for them to be provided not only with the other graces of the Spirit, but also certainly with wisdom, for without it that task cannot be properly carried out. They may thus be on their guard not only against the impostures and frauds of those who are far too inclined to begging, and suck up what was needed for the brethren who were in extreme poverty, but also against the calumnies [slanders] of those who are constantly making disparaging remarks, even if there is no occasion for doing so. For as well as being full of difficulties that office is also exposed to unjustified complaints.[3]

NOT DOUBLE-TONGUED: INTEGRITY OF SPEECH

When I was a boy, my father drummed an old saying into my head: "A man is no better than his word." How true! Nothing destroys Christian community like deceit. So a servant entrusted with the care of needy people must, first of all, be sincere and trustworthy.

Scholars have different opinions concerning the exact meaning of "double-tongued." J. N. D. Kelly says that it signifies "saying one thing to one man and a different thing to the next."[4] Whatever its exact meaning, the term plainly prohibits any kind of manipulative, insincere, or deceitful speech. Behind a deceitful tongue is a deceitful mind. Positively, the term emphasizes integrity of speech, sincerity, and truthfulness.

Far too many Christian leaders have demonstrated that their word cannot be trusted, especially when it concerns money. They are self-deceived double talkers. According to God's Word, they don't qualify to be deacons. A deacon must be a man of his word. He must mean what he says; his "yes" must mean yes and his "no" must mean no (2 Corinthians 1:17-20).

Not Addicted to Much Wine:
Above Reproach in the Use of Alcohol

The Bible contains many warnings against the potential dangers of wine and strong drink (Isaiah 5:11,22; Proverbs 20:1; 23:30-35; Hosea 4:11). Drunkenness is sin, and persistently drunken people require church discipline. (See 1 Corinthians 5:11; 6:9,10; Galatians 5:21; Ephesians 5:18; 1 Peter 4:3.) So a person in a position of trust over other people can't have a drinking problem.

Scripture specifically warns leaders about the dangers of alcohol:

> It is not for kings, O Lemuel,
> It is not for kings to drink wine,
> Or for rulers to desire strong drink,
> Lest they drink and forget what is decreed,
> And pervert the rights of all the afflicted (Proverbs 31:4,5;
> cf. Leviticus 10:8,9; Isaiah 28:1,7,8; 56:9-12).

97

Drunkenness has ruined countless lives. It is commonly reported that nearly half of the murders, suicides, and accidental deaths in America are related to alcohol. One in four families has some problem with alcohol, making alcohol one of the largest health problems in America. The misery and heartbreak that alcoholism has caused multitudes of families is beyond imagination. It reduces life expectancy, breaks up families, and destroys people financially. It's a moral and spiritual problem of the greatest magnitude. No one who has worked with the people or families who are its victims joke about its destructive power.

We must not be naive or silent about alcoholism among church leaders. Deacons work with people, often those who are troubled. If a deacon has a drinking problem, he will lead people astray and bring reproach upon the church. His overindulgence will interfere with spiritual growth and service, and it could lead to more degrading sins. A man who seeks to demonstrate the love of Christ to others must control this area of his life.

Finally, note carefully that Paul actually says, "...not addicted [given to] to *much* wine" (italics added). Plainly this is not an absolute prohibition against drinking wine. It is a prohibition against the abuse of wine (or any other substance) that would damage a man's testimony and work for God.

NOT FOND OF SORDID GAIN:
NOT GREEDY FOR MONEY, FINANCIAL INTEGRITY

Paul certainly had false teachers in mind (1 Timothy 6:5; Titus 1:11) when he listed this qualification. It's natural to wonder if he had Judas in mind, for Judas best illustrates what "fond of sordid gain" means. As the treasurer of our Lord's band of disciples, Judas spoke as if he cared for the poor, but he actually cared for money. After Mary poured her expensive perfume on the Lord in worship, Judas sanctimoniously complained, "'Why was this perfume not sold for three hundred denarii, and given to poor people?'" John, however, explains Judas' real concern: "Now he said this, not because he was concerned about the poor, but because he was a thief, and as he had the money box, he used to pilfer what was put into it" (John 12:5,6).

Throughout the Bible, there are examples of and warnings against people who use their religious offices to achieve financial gain at the expense of others. (See Numbers 22-24; 1 Samuel 2:13-17; 2 Kings 5:20-27; Isaiah 22:15-25.) Our Lord confronted this serious problem while on earth. He blatantly accused the scribes and Pharisees of stealing from "widows' houses" (Luke 20:47a) and charged that they were "full of robbery" (Luke 11:39b). Twice He had to clean out the temple of God, which had become a merchandise mart:

> And Jesus entered the temple and cast out all those who were buying and selling in the temple.... And He said to them, "It is written, 'My house shall be called a house of prayer'; but you are making it a robbers' den" (Matthew 21:12a,13).

Exposing the motives of the religious leaders, Luke declares that they "were lovers of money" (Luke 16:14a). In direct contrast, God states, "Let your character be free from the love of money..." (Hebrews 13:5a).

Deacons handle money—other people's money, the church's money—and where money is there are always problems. Money is an irresistible magnet for many people. They are deceived by the burning passion of greed. Such people seek out positions that provide access to money, although they do not admit their true desires. Such people may not actually steal cash. Instead, they may misdirect church funds to their own so-called "ministry expenses": gas, car repairs, meals, travel, and home. (Contrast Nehemiah 5:14-18.) This still is wrongfully seeking gain that belongs to others; it is "sordid gain."

So we must carefully examine a man's financial integrity before he is chosen to be a deacon. A person who has a problem with greed, stealing, or making bad financial dealings isn't a good candidate for the diaconate. Our goal is for all our shepherds and deacons to be able to say, as Samuel the godly judge of Israel did:

> "Here I am; bear witness against me before the Lord and His anointed. Whose ox have I taken, or whose donkey have I taken, or whom have I defrauded? Whom have I oppressed, or from whose hand have I taken a bribe to blind my eyes with it? I will restore it to you" (1 Samuel 12:3).

HOLDING TO THE MYSTERY OF THE FAITH WITH A CLEAR CONSCIENCE: A MAN'S LIFE AND DOCTRINE MUST MATCH

This final qualification means that a deacon's life must be consistent with Christian doctrine. "The Christian maintains a clear conscience by living in harmony with the truths unveiled in God's Word," states Lawrence O. Richards in the *Expository Dictionary of Bible Words*.[5]

A Christian can't hold to the faith with a pure conscience and live in sexual immorality, pilfer money, hate a brother, divorce a Christian spouse, or mix falsehood with the gospel. The New Testament never allows people to separate life and doctrine. Whenever we knowingly act in a way that is contrary to God's Word and do not seek His forgiveness, we defile our conscience. Every time we violate our conscience, we weaken its convicting power and make sin and hypocrisy easier to commit. Therefore, a Christian whose inconsistent, hypocritical life belies biblical truth can't be a deacon.

The conscience is our self-judging faculty or "moral self-consciousness," to use George W. Knight, III's terminology.[6] "Its basic meaning," writes J. N. D. Kelly, "is man's inner awareness of the moral quality of his own actions."[7] Because the conscience both judges and guides a believer, we are not to go against it. For Christians, conscience, faith, and the Holy Spirit are all interrelated (Romans 9:1; 14:22,23). The false teachers in the church at

Ephesus defiled their consciences by trusting in their prideful thoughts and base desires rather than in God's sound revelation. In the end, they shipwrecked their faith and all who followed them (1 Timothy 1:19,20; 2 Timothy 2:18).

The expression "mystery of the faith" is a beautiful, grand way of referring to Christianity's distinctive truths. In the New Testament, "mystery" means "revealed secret"—a divine plan or purpose previously hidden and unaccessible to people but now revealed by God and proclaimed to all who will believe. W. E. Vine, in *Expository Dictionary of New Testament Words,* writes:

> In the N.T. it denotes, not the mysterious (as with the Eng. word), but that which, being outside the range of unassisted natural apprehension, can be made known only by Divine revelation, and is made known in a manner and at a time appointed by God, and to those only who are illumined by His Spirit. In the ordinary sense a mystery implies knowledge withheld; its Scriptural significance is truth revealed.[8]

According to 1 Timothy 3:9, deacons must hold to the "mystery of the faith" with a clear conscience. What is "the mystery of the faith?" The answer is found in the word *faith.* Faith defines the content of the mystery. For example, in other passages, Paul speaks of the "mystery of God," "mystery of Christ," "mystery of the gospel," "mystery of His will," and "mystery of godliness." Here he says, "...the mystery of the faith." Faith explains what this mystery is. "The faith" means the entire body of Christian doctrine, Christianity's distinctive truths.[9] The "mystery" is defined, then, as the objective body of truth of which the Christian faith is comprised. The *New English Bible* renders this phrase, "...the deep truths of our faith." We can, therefore, translate "the mystery of the faith" as "the revealed secrets of the Christian faith."

Since God has divulged the glorious, divine secrets of redemption to us, an awesome responsibility rests on every Christian to live consistently and obediently according to these truths.

A Christian can bring disgrace on God's wonderful revelations by sinful, hypocritical behavior. Or, a Christian can make the message of Christianity attractive to unbelievers by demonstrating behavior that fits the truths of the faith (Titus 2:10). A deacon must hold steadfastly to the Christian faith and live consistently with its beliefs.

Biblical commentator, Homer Kent, summarizes this qualification by saying:

> The great truths of the faith are not to be held as theological abstractions, but are to be properly employed in daily life. To hold the mystery of the faith in a pure conscience is so to live in the light of Christian truth that the enlightened conscience will have no cause to condemn. A pure conscience indicates a pure life.[10]

Chapter 9

Qualification Demands Examination

And let these also first be tested; then let them serve as deacons if they are beyond reproach.
1 Timothy 3:10

Throughout this book, we have talked about deacons' qualifications. Now we come to an equally important subject—the examination of deacons. Five qualifications for deacons have been laid down in 1 Timothy 3:8,9, but they are just empty words without the requirement in verse 10 to examine a candidate's fitness for office. The text plainly states that no one can serve as a deacon until "first" tested (examined) and approved.

According to verse 9, a deacon candidate must hold "to the mystery of the faith with a clear conscience." We all know that a person may think his conscience is clean and yet be deceived. We all suffer from a certain amount of blindness to our sins. But the more blind we are to our sins, the more harm we may do to others. Sharing perfect wisdom from above, Paul interrupts his list of specific qualifications to add this essential requirement that makes

103

all the others meaningful: "And let these also first be tested; then let them serve as deacons...."

The word "also" must not go unnoticed. It is important to the development of Paul's thinking in this section. The words "And...these also" alert us to something slightly different from, but equally essential to, the five character requirements just listed. The inspired writer now emphasizes that the deacons must be tested in the same way that the overseer-elders must be tested. Thus "And...these also" refers back to the overseers (bishops) mentioned in the previous section (3:1-7).[1] Translators of the *New English Bible* took the liberty to add the term "bishops" (overseers) to the translation in order to make this point perfectly clear: "No less than bishops, they must first undergo a scrutiny, and if there is no mark against them, they may serve."

We know from 1 Timothy 5:24,25 that the character and work of all prospective elders was to be carefully assessed by others. So we should not be surprised that Paul lays down a similar requirement for deacons. We have a tendency to think that the biblical standards for deacons require less enforcement than the standards for elders. But that is a serious mistake.

This is precisely where many churches fail. The confirmation process of a prospective deacon takes time and effort, and many churches are too busy with other matters to make the effort. (Perhaps the church in Ephesus was also too busy to examine thoroughly its deacons and elders.) However, it is as important for deacons to be examined regarding their fitness for office as it is for elders. An unfit deacon can cause many problems in the church and hurt innocent people.

THE EXAMINATION PROCESS

The passive imperative form of the verb that is rendered "let these...be tested" stresses the necessity for testing a prospective deacon. It is not an option. A man cannot appoint himself to the diaconate. Every prospective deacon must be evaluated by others who must examine his Christian character in light of God's standards.

The word "tested" is derived from the Greek word *dokimazō*. Richard Trench claims that "in *dokimazein*...lies ever the notion of proving a thing whether it be worthy *to be received* or not...."[2] In ancient Greek literature, this word was sometimes used in relation to testing a person's credentials for public office.[3] In our present context, it means "the examination of candidates for the diaconate."[4] The idea here is for others to officially examine, evaluate, and scrutinize the prospective deacon's character. Just as medical doctors are officially examined before they are licensed, so prospective shepherds and deacons are to be examined in light of God's requirements (1 Timothy 3:2-12) before they can take office.

But how is a prospective deacon actually to be examined? What are the procedures? For important reasons, the New Testament is silent on these specific matters, just as it is silent regarding specific procedures for administering the Lord's Supper and baptism. (There is no book in the New Testament like the Old Testament book of Leviticus.) This lack of specific procedures has provided ample territory for many self-defeating church battles.

We must remember that the silence of the New Testament on these kinds of details is highly instructive. The church of Jesus Christ is a Spirit-indwelt body of redeemed people who have been called from all nations. One reason for the absence of detailed instructions is to allow each congregation the freedom and flexibility to adapt God's wonderful truths to the culture in which it ministers. The local Christian assembly is to be culturally relevant, yet radically different. (Consider 1 Corinthians 9:19-23.) God marvelously designed the local church to be adaptable to every culture and to function in any life situation, especially persecution.

The absence of detailed regulations and legal codes in the New Testament is also a practical expression of the glorious liberty and freedom into which Christians have been brought (Galatians 5:1,13). We are Spirit empowered and Spirit led. Thus, in dependence on the Spirit of the living God within the bounds of His Word, we can confidently seek His help in implementing His truths in relevant ways. So a spiritually alive church is always marked by fresh creativity in evangelism, worship, music, discipleship, and expressions of love. Yet many churches slowly strangle their spiritual vitality because they will not change their outmoded traditions and comfortable ways.

Of course, divine, biblical principles should not be changed in order to be culturally acceptable. To do that is to betray both our God and our culture. Specific Christian principles are to distinguish the local church of Jesus Christ (and this book touches on a number of them). To abandon biblically revealed principles would be to lose our Christian distinctiveness and displease our Lord Jesus Christ.

Because 1 Timothy 3:10 provides no detailed procedures for examination of deacon candidates, different churches will develop different procedures. The express requirements of Scripture are that: (1) the deacon candidate meet all biblical qualifications; (2) the deacon candidate must be examined as to those qualifications; and (3) no deacon be appointed to office in a hasty, careless manner (1 Timothy 5:22). Although detailed procedures are left to the discernment of the local church and its shepherds, certain key, general elements should be part of any examination or confirmation process. Let us briefly examine some of these elements for orderly examination.

Overseers Should Direct the Process

According to 1 Timothy 3:1 and Titus 1:5, a local church must appoint overseers. By definition, overseers must oversee the direction of the church. In 1 Timothy 5:17, the elders (overseers) are the ones, as F. F. Bruce translates, "who direct the affairs of the church."[5] The word "direct" is the Greek word *prohistēmi*, which signifies leading, managing, directing, and superintending. So in vital matters as important as examining and appointing deacons, the overseer-elders should direct the entire examination process.

If not, disorder and mismanagement will ensue, and people will be hurt.

In practical reality, if the shepherds do not take the initiative in these matters, little will take place in their church. The shepherds have the authority, position, and knowledge to move the church forward. They know its needs, and they know the people. Furthermore, the shepherds are responsible to decide if additional deacons are needed and to initiate the process of selecting them.

The Congregation Must Be Actively Involved

Because the shepherds are to take the lead in examination procedures does not suggest that the congregation is left out of the evaluation process. Absolutely not! New Testament elders should never act like dictators, bureaucrats, or a ruling oligarchy. Rather, they actively lead as loving shepherds among God's people. They must listen to, consult with, and seek the wisdom of their fellow believers. A good shepherding body also wants an educated, involved congregation, not a passive one. The appointed deacons will serve the congregation, so the people must have a voice in evaluating them.

The context of the passage before us is to relate general instruction to the whole church (2:1-3:16), not just to the shepherds. Therefore, everyone in the church is to know these qualifications and is also obligated to see that these biblical instructions are implemented. Some people in the congregation may have information about a prospective deacon that the shepherds do not have, so their input in the evaluation process is essential, regardless of how that process is carried out.

If objections or accusations are voiced as to a deacon candidate's character, the shepherds should find out if the accusations are scripturally based. If not, the objections or accusations should be ignored. No candidate should be refused office because of someone's personal bias. *People must give scriptural reasons for their objections. This evaluation process is not a popularity contest or freewheeling election. It is a testing of character according to the light of Scripture.* If even one person in the congregation has a verified scriptural objection, the prospective deacon should be declared unfit for office—even if everyone else approves. *God's standards alone govern God's house, not group popularity.*

According to 1 Timothy 3:10, the standard for approving a deacon is that he be found to be "beyond reproach," which means unaccused. This means the character and conduct of such a person, even under formal censure, is free from justifiable accusation. In other words, the candidate has been examined according to biblical qualifications (1 Timothy 3:8-12) and nothing has been found against him.

Please note that this does not mean the candidate does not have faults or imperfections. We all do. Being "beyond reproach" is related to the qualifications for office only. Thus the qualified deacon is worthy of respect, truthful, self- controlled in the use of wine, lives a consistent Christian life, and is a faithful husband and father.

Questioning and Instructing the Deacon Candidate

During a meeting (or several meetings) with the prospective deacon, the shepherds and/or others of the congregation should inquire about his beliefs, interests, family, and commitment of time. Furthermore, they should clarify to the candidate what work he will be expected to do.

Overseers Should Publicly Approve and Install Deacons

After the shepherds give their final approval, the candidate should be publicly installed into office. The fact that the congregation in Jerusalem brought their chosen men to the apostles indicates that they sought the apostles' approbation (Acts 6:6).

The Process Should Be Bathed in Prayer

Finally, all procedures and details concerning this important decision must be bathed in prayer. People must pray for spiritual insight, guidance, and unbiased judgment. They must desire God's will and pleasure, not their own.

Sadly, too many churches expend the least amount of time and effort in examining prospective deacons or shepherds. A friend told me that in his church the pastor invites all the members to assemble in the church basement once a year, after a Sunday-evening service, to elect deacons. After everyone gathers in front of a blackboard, the chairman of the deacons asks for nominations to the diaconate. Several names are suggested and quickly voted on. The new deacons are then installed, and the pastor closes the meeting in prayer. The entire process takes half an hour. There is no consideration of scriptural qualifications, no prayer, and no time to fully examine the nominated deacons. It is a simple matter of "let's get some people on the board."

Thoughtless, lazy, and prayerless procedures like these weaken our churches and demean the diaconate and eldership. Evaluating a deacon's fitness for office should be done thoughtfully, patiently, and biblically.

PUBLIC RECOGNITION OF THE OFFICE OF DEACON

The word "first" in 1 Timothy 3:10 informs us that there is an order to observe when appointing deacons. The text reads, "And let these also *first* be tested; *then* let them serve as deacons..." (italics added). A prospective deacon's character must first be examined according to God's standards (1 Timothy 3:8-12). Only after the candidate is approved can he be officially and publicly recognized (or installed) as a deacon. He then remains a deacon until he no longer desires the work of the diaconate or disqualifies himself according to the biblical requirements. To arbitrarily limit deacons to a two- or three-year term of service demeans the diaconate to board status and frustrates a man's God-given desire to serve the Lord's people. If a deacon needs time off to rest, that is a different matter, but the decision should be left to the individual, not dictated by unbiblical tradition.

The fact that a man does not serve as a deacon until he is first examined and approved shows that not everyone who serves in the local church is a deacon. I have heard people say, "If you are serving the church, then you are a deacon." That is not accurate. It is true that we all are to be servants of one another. Yet there is, in the New Testament, a special office of servant for which one must qualify and be approved. That is what the text before us teaches.

As to the deacon's official installation into office, the New Testament gives no detailed instructions or regulations. Likewise, the Old Testament says nothing about the elders' installation into office. Apparently the inspired writers of Scripture were not greatly concerned about this matter.

In contrast, when appointing the Old Testament priest, there was an elaborate and detailed ceremonial procedure. There were special sacrifices that had to be offered, special washings, ceremonial garments, prescribed actions on certain days, and anointings with holy oil (Exodus 28:40-29:41). No one could even slightly deviate from these prescribed laws of God.

However, the New Testament deacons and shepherds are not anointed priests like Aaron and his sons (Leviticus 8:12). Nor are the deacons and shepherds installed into a special priestly office or sacred clerical order. Instead, they are assuming positions of service or leadership among God's people. We should not sacralize these positions more than the writers of Scripture do. The vocabulary the New Testament writers chose expresses simple appointment to office. Therefore, to speak of ordaining deacons or shepherds is as confusing and meaningless as speaking of ordaining judges or politicians.[6]

Although the Seven mentioned in Acts 6 were appointed to the business of providing relief for the poor and were not appointed to holy priesthood or clerical orders, an official, public installation still took place. So Acts 6 gives us general guidance and wisdom that will help us install deacons. The apostles—the church overseers— officially and publicly placed the Seven into their new position by prayer and the laying on of hands (Acts 6:3,6).

This was their way to recognize people who were being appointed or commissioned for special work (Acts 6:6; 13:3; 1 Timothy 4:14; 5:22). This is an important principle for the congregation and those who are being recognized or commissioned to understand. The church is not a secret society. Important issues such as installing elders and deacons must be done in public. The congregation needs to be informed about who its leaders are, and the leaders need the prayers and affirmation of the congregation.

Chapter 10

Qualifications for Wives Who Assist Their Deacon Husbands

> **Women must likewise be dignified, not malicious gossips, but temperate, faithful in all things.**
>
> **1 Timothy 3:11**

As we have discovered, Paul lists five character qualifications for deacons in 1 Timothy 3:8,9:

- Men of dignity
- Not double-tongued
- Not addicted to much wine
- Not fond of sordid gain
- Holding to the mystery of the faith with a clear conscience

After giving these qualifications, he insists that each candidate for deaconship be publicly examined and approved before serving as a deacon: "And let these also first be tested; then let them serve as deacons if they are beyond reproach" (3:10).

Then, in verse 11, by means of the word "likewise," Paul introduces a new class of people who are closely associated with deacons. Paul lists four character qualifications for this group of people, indicating that this third group also must serve the church in some way. People in this group must be:

• Dignified
• Not malicious gossips
• Temperate
• Faithful in all things

Finally, in verse 12, Paul resumes his list of personal character requirements for deacons: "Let deacons be husbands of only one wife, and good managers of their children and their own households."

To help visualize what we have just stated, below is 1 Timothy 3:8-13 divided into four sections.

Deacons [male] likewise must be men of dignity, not double-tongued, or addicted to much wine or fond of sordid gain, but holding to the mystery of the faith with a clear conscience (verses 8,9).

And let these also first be tested; then let them serve as deacons if they are beyond reproach (verse 10).

Gynaikas [women/wives] must likewise be dignified, not malicious gossips, but temperate, faithful in all things (verse 11).

Let deacons [male] be husbands of only one wife, and good managers of their children and their own households (verse 12).

Who is this new group of people called *gynaikas* (pronounced goo-NAI-kas, the accusative plural of *gynē*)? In Greek, *gynē* (pronounced, goo-NAY) is the standard word for an adult

113

woman or wife. Only the context determines if *gynē* should be translated as "woman" or "wife." Thus, *gynaikas* are either (1) women who are deacons, (2) women who assist deacons, or (3) wives who assist their deacon husbands. Although each view has its problems, the interpretation we seek most adequately explains all of the following key interpretive issues of the text.

The Meaning of the Word Gynaikas *(Women/Wives)*

Certainly in this passage Paul isn't referring to Christian women in general, as he does in 1 Timothy 2:9. In the middle of a context regarding deacons' qualifications and church office, it is most unlikely that he'd start talking about general character qualifications for all the women of the church. This would senselessly interrupt an otherwise orderly passage. Since these women are not Christian women in general, we'd expect Paul to use a modifying word or phrase that clearly identifies who these *gynaikas* are. For example, he might have used "women who help," "women who are deacons," or "their women" (wives). But he doesn't. Paul simply writes *gynaikas* with no modifier, which presents a problem of interpretation.

The Placement of Verse 11

The position of verse 11, which is wedged in the middle of a context on male deacons, appears to be awkward. Why does Paul list four qualifications for certain women in the middle of his instruction on male deacons' qualifications? Don't these women deserve a separate paragraph of their own after or before the instruction on male deacons?

The Issue of Women Officers

Paul's teaching on the women's role in the local church (1 Timothy 2:9-15) is intimately tied with his instruction on over-seers and deacons:

Likewise, I want women [Greek, *gynaikas*] to adorn themselves with proper clothing...[and] by means of good works, as befits women making a claim to godliness.... *But I do not allow a woman to teach or exercise authority over a man, but to remain quiet.* For it was Adam who was first created, and then Eve. And it was not Adam who was deceived, but the woman being quite deceived, fell into transgression (2:9*a*,10, 12-14; italics added).

First Timothy 2:9-15 and 3:1-13 must never be isolated from each other or be allowed to contradict each other. They are inseparably woven together. Therefore, 1 Timothy 2:9-15 is part of the larger context to which 1 Timothy 3:11 belongs and must be considered when interpreting 1 Timothy 3:11.[1]

Whether the Adverb "Likewise" in Verse 11 Indicates Another Church Office.

The word "likewise" in verse 11 signals that Paul is introducing a new class of people: *gynaikas*—women/wives. This new group is distinct from, yet compared with, the male deacons mentioned previously. Some commentators think that "likewise" necessitates another church office similar to the ones preceding.

With these critical interpretive issues in mind, let us examine three possible interpretations of 1 Timothy 3:11.

WOMEN WHO ARE DEACONS

Many sound Bible students interpret *gynaikas* to mean "women who are deacons." The strongest reason for thinking these women are deacons is that the entire context is about church officers, thus women introduced by "likewise," parallel with verse 8, would appear to be women officers who are similar to deacons. This view, however, raises the perplexing question of why Paul would write *gynaikas* if he means "women deacons."

115

Why Gynaikas *and not* tas Diakonous

Patrick Fairbairn (1805-1875), a Scottish theologian and commentator who defends the view of women deacons, honestly admits this is difficult to explain. In his classic commentary on the Pastoral Epistles, Fairbairn confesses, "It still is somewhat strange, however, that the general term *women* (*gynaikas*) is employed, and not the specific *deaconesses* (*tas diakonous*), which would have excluded all uncertainty as to the meaning."[2]

In the Greek language of New Testament times, Koine Greek, there was no special word for *deaconess*. The first recorded instance of the Greek word, *diakonissa* ("deaconess"), appears to be in the nineteenth canon of the First Council of Nicaea (A.D. 325). However, the Greek noun *diakonos*, although masculine in form is among a select number of second declension nouns that can be either masculine or feminine. Thus the masculine form can apply to women. There is no special feminine form such as *diakonē*.

To illustrate this point, in Romans 16:1 Paul refers to a woman named Phoebe as *diakonos*. He writes, "I commend to you our sister Phoebe, who is a servant [*diakonon*] of the church which is at Cenchrea." If, for the sake of argument, we say that Phoebe was a deacon as many commentators claim, then obviously Paul had no reluctance in calling her a "deacon," *diakonos*. (As to whether Phoebe was a deacon or not, the text in Romans 16 is ambiguous.[3] There are not enough clear indicators from the text to determine if *diakonos* simply means a caring servant in the general sense or a deacon in the official sense.) Therefore, if women were part of the diaconate in the church at Ephesus, they would also be called deacons, *diakonoi*, like their male counterparts.

The question then is, if Paul is singling out women deacons in verse 11, why does he use the ambiguous and general word *gynaikas*, and not *diakonoi* with the feminine article—*tas diakonous* ("women deacons")?

In referring to the two previous officers, Paul uses specific titles of office: "overseer" (verse 2) and "deacons" (verse 8,12). So why doesn't he again use a specific title to identify who he means—*especially if they are church officers?* Furthermore, since *diakonos* can be either masculine or feminine, shouldn't we expect *diakonoi* in verse 8 to cover both male and female deacons? Therefore it would be unnecessary for Paul to add verse 11, which says the same thing as verses 8,9. Let us look at this problem more closely.

In English, for example, we speak of the "minister" or "pastor" of a church, but today that person may be either male or female. We don't call a woman minister or pastor a "ministeress" or "pastoress". We say minister or pastor. The same thing is true of the word *nurse*. A nurse may be either male or female. We have no special form to distinguish male or female nurses. The same situation exists with the Greek word *diakonos*.[4]

Why, after listing five qualifications for "deacons" that could include males or females, does Paul in verse 11 repeat nearly the same qualifications for women deacons? That would be like saying that all nurses must attend four years of college and then singling out male nurses and repeating that male nurses must attend four years of college with a slightly different terminology. The required four years of college applies to all nurses, male or female.

If Paul is indeed singling out female deacons in verse 11, we then should expect him to add some uniquely important qualifications for women deacons. That is not the case. Instead, as all commentators agree, Paul lists nearly the same qualifications as those listed in verses 8-9. So, to understand *gynaikas* as referring to women deacons leaves us with formidable unanswered questions.

The Placement of Verse 11

A second problem that confronts the view of women deacons is the placement of verse 11 in the middle of a paragraph on male deacons' qualifications. Verse 11, if referring to women deacons, seems to be an awkward interjection of thought in a section that is basically well ordered. It would seem more orderly if verse 11 were placed at the end of verse 12.

Particularly arresting is the use of the word "deacons" in verse 12, which alerts the reader that Paul is resuming his subject of the deacons' personal qualifications. His insertion of the word "deacons" makes it appear that verse 11 refers to someone other than women deacons.

Although these questions are somewhat problematic, they could be explained by Paul's unique style of writing. It is not uncommon for Paul to interject related ideas into his flow of thought as they come to mind (1 Timothy 5:23). So the placement of verse 11, although problematic, is not a decisive argument against the interpretation that *gynaikas* refers to women deacons.

The Presence of Women Officers

Finally, those who believe in women deacons must reconcile the idea of women officials in the church with Paul's prohibition against women taking authority over men in the church. According to the New Testament, deacons hold an official position of authority, in close association with the overseers. Deacons do not simply provide private, individual help to others—something all Christian men and women are to do. Deacons guide and direct the entire church's overall welfare ministry. They make decisions that affect the whole church body. They are the church's official managers or representatives of mercy ministries.

Since both offices, eldership and deaconship, demand the exercise of authority that extends over the entire local church, an argument can be made that both offices are restricted to males. The idea of women deacons, then, conflicts with the entire context, particularly 1 Timothy 2:12, which states "But I do not allow a woman to...exercise authority over a man...." Paul's restriction on women having authority over men in the local church (1 Timothy 2:12) raises serious doubts about 1 Timothy 3:11 referring to women being deacons.

One answer is to say that women deacons serve only women

and that male deacons serve only men. But this is pure conjecture and contrary to the example of Acts 6. In Acts 6, seven men were appointed to provide for and protect the Jerusalem church's helpless widows. Does this not fit the biblical picture of what mature men, by nature of their God-created masculinity, are called to do—protect, lead, and provide for women?[5]

(Because of widespread male abuse of women and conceptual distortions of the biblical model for masculinity and femininity, I must qualify the previous statement. In God's design, men are to protect, lead, and provide for women, but never in a superior, dominating, selfish, or belittling way. Men are to lead in a responsible, sacrificial, and loving way, like Christ does the Church, Ephesians 5:22-33.)

There were male deacons in churches during the apostolic period. Indeed, in the passage before us, the only persons clearly called deacons are men. It is obvious from the context that the official title "deacons" in verse 8 refers to male deacons only (verses 8-10). Paul addresses women in verse 11, and in verse 12, where the official title "deacons" appears a second time, he again addresses men. Paul requires that deacons be the "husbands of only one wife" and that they manage well "their children and their own households." So both times the word "deacons" appears in 1 Timothy 3:8-12, it applies only to men.

When we consider the evidence for women deacons, however, we do not find conclusive evidence for their existence during New Testament times. In the third century, a church order manual called the *Didascalia Apostolorum* ("Teaching of the Apostles," c. A.D. 230), which represented the eastern churches of the Roman Empire, contains the first positive identification of women deacons.[6] In a highly respected historical study entitled *The Ministry of Women in the Early Church,* French Roman Catholic scholar, Roger Gryson, concludes: "The beginnings of a feminine diaconate are indeed hidden in shadow and darkness, and difficult to perceive with any exactness."[7]

Moreover, even where the institution of deaconesses existed, it was never considered to be equal in status with the male diaconate. In the most scholarly and comprehensive study to date on deaconesses, Roman Catholic church historian, Aime George Martimort, demonstrates through painstaking analysis of all available literature that "...during all the time when the institution of deaconesses was a living institution, both the discipline and the liturgy of the churches insisted upon a very clear distinction between deacons and deaconesses."[8]

Therefore, those who postulate that verse 11 refers to women deacons are building this doctrine on quite uncertain ground. Indeed, this interpretation leaves us with a number of unanswered questions and problems. In light of the strengths of the following two interpretations, it seems that this is the weakest of the three views.

WOMEN WHO ASSIST DEACONS

An interpretation that better agrees with the facts and questions raised by 1 Timothy 3:11 is that Paul is referring to the "women who assist deacons." William Hendriksen, a biblical commentator and a leading proponent of this view, writes, "These women, are *the deacons' assistants* in helping the poor and needy, etc. These are *women who render auxiliary service*, performing ministries for which women are better adapted."[9] According to this view, Paul refers to this new group of people in verse 11 as *gynaikas* (women) precisely because they have no official title. They are not deacon officials. Moreover, this view eliminates any conflict with Paul's earlier assertions in 1 Timothy 2:12 about women not having authority over men.

These women are not deacons. Yet they are so closely associated with deacons that they can be addressed within the context of deacons. These women have functions to perform or there would be no need for them to be mentioned here or to be required to meet specific qualifications. What these women do is closely associated with what deacons do. We can easily conceive of the deacons' need for women helpers to assist widows and other needy women. Thus we would assume that these women work alongside the deacons as helpers.

Opponents of this view, however, insist that these women must be deacon officials because the conjunction "likewise" introduces a new category of officials like deacons or overseers. But this is pressing the word "likewise" too far. The use of "likewise" introduces a fresh category of people and compares them with the preceding group. It doesn't necessarily imply that women are official deacons. It could equally imply that these women assist deacons or are wives who assist their deacon husbands. The use of "likewise" actually works for all three views, but it would militate against the view of women in general.

Thus the interpretation "women who assist deacons" is quite possible. But the question of why *gynaikas* appears without any identifying words, such as "women assistants" or "women who help," when both overseers and deacons are clearly identified, remains. In spite of this issue, this interpretation is my second choice among the three.

WIVES WHO ASSIST THEIR DEACON HUSBANDS

The third interpretation explains *gynaikas* as being "wives of deacons." The word *gynaikas* is the standard Greek word for wives as well as for women. So if Paul means "wives" when he uses *gynaikas*, he makes perfectly good sense. We immediately know that he is talking about "wives."

This interpretation fits well with Paul's clear identification of overseers and deacons, the two previous groups of church officials. In verse 2 he uses the term "overseer." In verses 8 and 12 he uses the term "deacons." In verse 11, then, he identifies the group as "wives." In all three cases, Paul plainly identifies who he is referring to: overseers, deacons, and wives.

The Missing Pronoun

As simple as this interpretation appears, it still faces criticism. If Paul means to say "deacons' wives," why doesn't he add the possessive pronoun *their (autōn)* or the definite article (*tas*) to the word "women"? If he had only written "their women," we'd know, without a doubt, that he means deacons' wives.

Although the absence of the possessive pronoun *their* is often pointed out as a major drawback to this interpretation, its absence can be explained. First, the context surrounding *gynaikas* in verses 8-13 focuses on male deacons. To find *gynaikas* mentioned in the middle of this section on male deacons would naturally cause one to think of the wives of these male deacons. If no female deacons or women helped deacons in the church in Ephesus, the original readers would know that *gynaikas* could only be wives. Thus, the pronoun *their* would certainly be helpful to us, but *it is not necessary to the sentence grammatically, nor was it necessary to Paul's original readers.*

Furthermore, the absence of the pronoun *their* next to *gynaikas* can be explained stylistically. Verse 11 follows a parallel structure with verse 8. If you were to look at the Greek text, you'd see (or hear, if you were reading it aloud) that verse 11 almost exactly parallels verse 8. Here is how it appears in the Greek:

Verse 8: *diakonous hōsautōs semnous*
"Deacons likewise dignified"

Verse 11: *gynaikas hōsautōs semnas*
"Wives likewise dignified"

The rest of verse 11 also virtually parallels verses 8,9: "not malicious gossips" parallels "not double-tongued" in verse 8, "temperate" parallels "not...addicted to much wine" in verse 8, and "faithful in all things" parallels "holding to the mystery of the faith with a clear conscience" in verse 9. Thus verse 11 connects and parallels the structure and qualifications of verses 8 and 9. Paul, in his characteristic energetic and abbreviated style senses no need to add the pronoun or article. In the end, it's easier to explain the omission of the pronoun "their" than to explain why Paul uses the term "women" rather than *tas diakonous* or "women helpers."

Flow of Thought

The virtual repetition in verse 11 of the qualifications listed in verses 8 and 9 best fits with the interpretation that the women are the wives of deacons. If Paul is referring to female deacons or women who help deacons, we'd expect him to list additional and unique requirements, such as "wife of one man" or having obedient children. (See 1 Timothy 5:9,10.) Instead, he adds nothing new. If these women are wives, nothing new needs to be added. They must be like their husbands (verses 8,9). General guidelines regarding their domestic lives, which is of utmost importance to Paul, are included in verse 12 within the context of their deacon husbands.

This interpretation also fits best with the entire structure verses 8 through 13. In verses 8 and 9, Paul lists five character qualifications required of male deacons, and in verse 12 he adds domestic qualifications for deacons. Verses 10 and 11 form a break in the list of personal character qualifications, yet they also list important requirements for deacons: they must be examined and approved (like the overseers in verses 2 through 7), and their wives must be morally fit (like their deacon husbands in verses 8 and 9).

According to verse 10, deacons, like overseers, must be examined and approved before they can serve. The necessity to be examined and be found "beyond reproach" leads Paul to mention wives, those nearest the deacons, who also must play a role in diaconal service. These wives, like their deacon husbands, must be of similar moral character. So the examination process for deacons is to include the moral fitness of their wives.

Verse 11 then, like verses 8 through 10 and 12, contains another requirement necessary for deacons: their wives must be above reproach. Dr. George W. Knight, III, New Testament professor at Knox Theological Seminary and author of *Commentary on 1 Timothy* in the prestigious commentary series, *The New International Greek Testament Commentary*, states this point exceptionally well:

> If it is wives that are in view, then the verse fits here as another qualification necessary for one who would be a

deacon and who would conduct his ministry with his wife's assistance. Thus the wife's qualifications are part and parcel of his qualifications for the office of *diakonos*. And after giving the qualifications for the deacon's wife, Paul then goes on to the deacon's fidelity to his wife and his children and thereby completes the picture of his family life (v.12).[10]

Conclusion

If we accept the interpretation that the women are "deacons' wives," then we see that verse 11 is not an awkward interruption of thought in the midst of male deacons' requirements. Rather, it is a further requirement regarding deacons' fitness for office. Also, Paul's use of *gynaikas* as "wives" identifies exactly who he is referring to.[11]

It is interesting to observe how many English translations of the Bible favor the rendering "wives": *Authorized (King James) Version, New International Version, The New English Bible, The New Translation, The New Testament in Modern English, The Living Bible, Good News Bible (Today's English Version),* and *The Moffatt New Testament.*

Other translations, like the *New American Standard Bible,* translate *gynaikas* as "women," but that rendering is inadequate because it could be construed that Paul is referring to women in general—the very thing we know Paul is not saying. So translating *gynaikas* as "women" is misleading. If we want to translate *gynaikas* as "women," we must add a modifying word or phrase to avoid misunderstanding. The *Revised English Bible* does precisely that; it renders *gynaikas* as "women in this office." But if Paul uses *gynaikas* to mean "wives," we need to add nothing, although most English Bibles that translate *gynaikas* as wives add the pronoun "their" to make the point clear.

The interpretation "wives of deacons," moreover, avoids any conflict with Paul's earlier teaching on women not having authority over men in the church (1 Timothy 2:12). It affirms a male diaconate. Acts 6 supports this viewpoint. Here, in the appointing of the Seven, the apostles allowed only men to be selected. Yet what more opportune moment was there for the apostles to select at least a few women to a post of overall church management? But the apostles didn't. Did they fail? Absolutely not! As Christ's apostles who were led by the Holy Spirit, they did not fail.

It is highly instructive that in the establishment of the Seven, the Twelve required that men be selected. The Seven would constitute a major administrative body within the local church, supervising its funds and social welfare. The apostles themselves had performed this task. So, following their Lord's example of appointing only men to official leadership (as the male character of the apostolate itself demonstrates), they insisted on appointing men to this position.

Why couldn't women supervise the church's alms to its widows? Possibly the apostles required men because they knew that, in the Jewish culture of Palestine, people would respond better to men in a supervisory post than to women. A more likely reason, however, was due to God-ordained principles of manhood and womanhood (1 Corinthians 11:3,7; 1 Peter 3:1-7; 1 Timothy 2:12-14). We can be certain that God delights in women, as well as men, who perform charitable deeds (Luke 8:3; Acts 9:36). Luke, in both the Gospel of Luke and Acts, positively affirms the service of women.[12]

We can be certain that women in the early churches were involved in caring for the needy (Acts 9:36-39), as they should be in churches today. Christian women should always help others in need, evangelize, and serve Christ in other ways. However, in Acts 6, the apostles gave the overall leadership-supervision of the Jerusalem church's charity to men.

This decision was a matter of role differences between men and women in God's divine plan. It in no way suggests that Jesus Christ or His apostles discriminated against women. This thought is utterly repugnant. By choosing only men, our Lord was not accommodating Himself to human traditions or culture. In fearless confrontations and zeal for God's glory, Jesus challenged the most deep-seated traditions of His day. He also stated that all He said and did completely conformed to His Father's will (John 5:30). Before choosing the Twelve, He spent the night praying to

125

His Father (Luke 6:12,13). His choices were based on divine principles and the welfare of all His people.

As "modern" people, we might ask what the big deal is concerning women deacons, which shows that we do not fully understand that God cares deeply about the proper roles between women and men. The role differences between men and women are part of His fundamental design for the human race. In the Book of Genesis, God reveals that man and woman were created equal in some ways and different in others. (See Genesis 1:26-28; 2:7-25; 3:1-21.) The Christian home and local church must exemplify God's design for the equality and differences between the sexes, for biblical manhood and womanhood. Even in matters that might seem trivial, such as appointing women deacons, we must carefully maintain God's wise, creative design for men and women.

In trying to fit all the pieces of this textual puzzle together, we can conclude that this last interpretation allows all the pieces to fit together best. It is the simplest and most natural interpretation. Therefore, we can conclude that Paul is referring to wives who help their deacon husbands. We can also conclude from this passage of God-breathed, holy Scripture that a New Testament diaconate comprises only men.

QUALIFICATIONS FOR DEACONS' WIVES

Verse 11 should greatly encourage deacons, for what better help can a deacon have than a faithful wife? Describing the ideal wife, Scripture states:

> She extends her hand to the poor;
> And she stretches out her hands to the needy.
>   (Proverbs 31:20)

Therefore, when deacons are examined for office (verse 10), their wives must also be included in the examination process, since they serve (each to their own extent) as helpers to their deacon husbands. If a prospective deacon's wife isn't willing or able to help or doesn't meet the qualifications mentioned in verse 11, the prospective deacon isn't eligible at that time for office.

"But why," people often ask, "are the wives of deacons mentioned and not the wives of overseers?" The answer lies in the nature of the diaconate, which is not a teaching, governing office like the eldership. First Timothy 2:12 states, "But I do not allow a woman to teach or exercise authority over a man...." Pastor-elders (shepherds) teach and govern the whole church. Their wives are not to assist in the governing of the church.

The diaconate, on the other hand, provides loving service to the needy. Wives can assist their deacon husbands in this service without violating their God-ordained role in the local church. Indeed, at times their assistance may be demanded, as in cases involving the care of single mothers, children, and sick or elderly women. The wives are not deacon officials, however. They don't hold the office of deacon or any special title.

Why can we assume that the deacons' wives perform diaconal service? The answer is, there'd be no reason to list requirements for deacons' wives if they did not play a role in diaconal service. If Paul was only concerned with the behavior of the deacons' wives as it affected the deacons' qualification for office, then he has covered this in verse 12 with the requirement that deacons manage their households well. Precisely because the deacons' wives help in some way, Paul requires them to meet qualifications nearly identical to those of their husbands.

Paul lays down four requirements for deacons' wives in verse 11 that are similar to those found in 1 Timothy 3:8 and 9 that describe deacons:

- dignified
- not malicious gossips
- temperate
- faithful in all things

Let's examine these qualifications in more detail.

DIGNIFIED: A WOMAN WORTHY OF RESPECT

In 1 Timothy 3:8, deacons are required to be "men of dignity," that is, "worthy of respect." Now in verse 11, their "wives" likewise are required to be "dignified." (See verse 8.)

NOT MALICIOUS GOSSIPS: NOT SLANDEROUS, A WOMAN WHO CONTROLS HER TONGUE AND SPEAKS WISELY AND LOVINGLY

James, our Lord's half brother, sternly warns about the destructive power of the tongue.

> Now if we put bits into the horses' mouths so that they may obey us, we direct their entire body as well. Behold, the ships also, though they are so great and are driven by strong winds, are still directed by a very small rudder, wherever the inclination of the pilot desires. So also the tongue is a small part of the body, and yet it boasts of great things. Behold, how great a forest is set aflame by such a small fire! And the tongue is a fire, the very world of iniquity; the tongue is set among our members as that which defiles the entire body, and sets on fire the course of our life, and is set on fire by hell. For every species of beasts and birds, of reptiles and creatures of the sea, is tamed, and has been tamed by the human race. But no one can tame the tongue; it is a restless evil and full of deadly poison. (James 3:3-8).

The Greek word for "malicious gossips" is the same word for *devil* (in the singular). Here it is used as an adjective and thus means "slanderous" or "malicious talkers." Slander is the devil's work. It divides and hurts people. It destroys churches.

Malicious gossips create division, hatred, and suspicions. Malicious gossipers exhibit confused judgment and uncontrolled speech. They are controlled by unrestrained passions such as anger, jealousy, bitterness, wounded feelings, pride, or mental disorder. Such people often believe their own lies and accusations. Thus they are self-deceived. A malicious gossip spreads bad rumors, innuendos, criticisms, and lies about people.

Our God is the God of truth, justice, love, forbearance, and healing. The Old Testament law expressly forbids malicious gossip: "'You shall not go about as a slanderer among your people...'" (Leviticus 19:16). Solomon writes, "...He who spreads slander is a fool" (Proverbs 10:18). God blesses those who make peace with others. Therefore, He expects us to speak in love and truth, to heal wounds, and to mend broken relationships. A malicious talker, however, isn't concerned with fairness or healing, only with striking back, tearing down, hurting, venting anger, or entertaining evil thoughts. Therefore, a malicious gossip has no place in ministering to the neediest members of God's family.

TEMPERATE: POSSESSING STABLE CHARACTER, A WOMAN WHO HAS BALANCED JUDGMENT AND SELF-CONTROL

No English word is completely satisfactory for rendering the Greek word for "temperate" *(nēphalios)*. *Nēphalios* can mean sobriety in the use of wine. Here it is used to mean the mental and emotional sobriety of a person's overall character, speech, and conduct, which of course would include sobriety in the use of wine.[13] It denotes self-control, balanced judgment, and freedom from debilitating excesses. Negatively, *nēphalios* indicates an absence of any personal disorder that would distort a person's judgment or conduct. Positively, the word describes a person who is stable, circumspect, self-restrained, and clearheaded.

Wives who lack self-control and balanced mental perspective will inevitably undermine the deacons' service within the congregation. Lacking self-restraint, they will be easily snared by the devil or false teachers. It is essential that wives working in close association with the diaconate be mentally and emotionally stable and in control. They must be able to remain composed in all circumstances.

Faithful in All Things: A Faithful Christian Woman Who Can Be Relied on to Fulfill Her Christian Duty in Every Area of Life

When Paul wrote this passage, some women in Ephesus had already rebelled and even defected from the faith. A few women had "already turned aside to follow Satan" (1 Timothy 5:15). So it was important for deacons' wives to be "faithful in all things."

"Faithful in all things" is a beautiful phrase. Faithfulness is a key word in God's vocabulary. Some synonyms for "faithful" (in the passive sense) are "loyal," "trustworthy," "reliable," or "dependable." Of the Greek term for "faithful," the *Expository Dictionary of Bible Words* states, *"Pistos* portrays an unshakeable loyalty, which is displayed in a number of ways."[14]

When we examine the Bible, we see that faithfulness marked all the great men and women of God (Hebrews 3:5; Nehemiah 7:2; 9:8; Colossians 1:7). In the work of God, faithfulness is of significant importance (Psalm 101:6). It is the key measuring stick (1 Corinthians 4:2). Since God is absolutely faithful to His promises and His people, He expects His people to be faithful as well.

The world, however, is characterized by infidelity. It has no allegiance to anything but its own desires. Thus, God's final and rather comprehensive qualification for deacons' wives is not perfection or skilled work; it is faithfulness in all things—in all aspects of life.

We might expect Paul to say that these women must be faithful to God or to their families. Instead, he writes, "...faithful in all things." That means they are to be faithful in every relationship and sphere of life: in their commitment to Christ and His Word, in their duties to their families, in their witness to neighbors, and in their responsibilities to the family of God. Every aspect of their life is to be marked by faithfulness.

A woman who commits adultery or is flirtatious is untrustworthy. A woman who neglects her family because of selfish ambitions, or neglects God's people, or walks in disobedience to the Word of God is unfaithful. A fickle, selfish woman who changes her mind or breaks commitments to please her own whims is unreliable. As Solomon writes in Proverbs 25:19, "Like a bad tooth and an unsteady foot is confidence in a faithless man [or woman] in time of trouble."

In helping their deacon husbands in this crucially significant ministry, these women have an important responsibility to fill. Thus we must insist that they, like their husbands, be biblically qualified. Let us not be indifferent to God's instruction regarding deacons' wives.

Chapter 11

Family Requirements for Deacons

> Let deacons be husbands of only one wife, and good
> managers of their children and their own households.
>
> **1 Timothy 3:12**

Paul did not complete his discussion of deacons with his list of qualifications for deacons' wives. By means of the phrase, "Let deacons be...," Paul alerts his readers that he is resuming the list of deacons' personal qualifications. He then names two final requirements that relate to the deacons' family life. To God, the deacons' marital and family life is of supreme importance. Indeed, family issues are matters of life and death to the local church.

THE NEED FOR MARITAL PURITY
AND FAMILY QUALIFICATIONS

In the first books of the Bible, God warned His people against the corrupt, debase, sexual practices of the surrounding heathen nations. He commanded His people to be separate from these nations and to uphold marital fidelity and sexual purity. This also is a principle of first order for the local church. This principle cannot be violated without the deadliest of consequences, as the Old Testament amply demonstrates.

Knowing this, Satan employs his full arsenal of seductive devices to adulterate the marriages of God's people. In Genesis 6, we learn that when the godly family of Seth (Genesis 5) intermarried with the godless line of Cain, the resulting generations wreaked such havoc on the earth that God had to destroy them by the flood.[1] Moses records:

> Now it came about, when men began to multiply on the face of the land, and daughters were born to them, that the sons of God [God's people] *saw that the daughters of men* [godless people] *were beautiful;* and they took wives for themselves, whomever they chose.... Then the Lord saw that the wickedness of man was great on the earth, and that every intent of the thoughts of his heart was only evil continually (Genesis 6:1,2,5; italics added).

In the Book of Leviticus, Moses lists in detail all the sexual sins of the godless nations that would surround the nation of Israel (Leviticus 18:1-23). The children of God, warns Moses, must never practice such sins or they, too, will be destroyed:

> "Do not defile yourselves by any of these things [the depraved sexual practices of the heathen]; for by all these the nations which I am casting out before you have become defiled.... Thus you are to keep My charge, that you do not practice any of the abominable customs which have been practiced before you, so as not to defile yourselves with them; I am the Lord your God" (Leviticus 18:24,30).

Although the evil soothsayer, Balaam, couldn't curse Israel for King Balak, he told Balak how to destroy God's people.

FAMILY REQUIREMENTS FOR DEACONS

Balaam's secret was that the sexual immorality of the depraved Moabite fertility cult could corrupt God's people (Numbers 25:1-9; 31:16). Balaam's cunning plan worked, and it still works today (1 Corinthians 10:8-11; Revelation 2:14). The *New International Version* reads:

> While Israel was staying in Shittim, the men began to indulge in sexual immorality with Moabite women, who invited them to the sacrifices to their gods. The people ate and bowed down before these gods. So Israel joined in worshiping the Baal of Peor. And the Lord's anger burned against them (Numbers 25:1-3).

Satan later shattered the nation of Israel through King Solomon's lust for many women. The Scripture tells us, "Now King Solomon loved many foreign women.... When Solomon was old, his wives turned his heart away after other gods" (1 Kings 11:1*a*,4*a*). As a result of Solomon's sin, God's people divided into two rival kingdoms. Balaam's old plan of action worked again. (Also read Ezra 9:1-4, for another example of Israelite leaders who contaminated God's people through marital defilement.)

Tragically, most Christian denominations have learned absolutely nothing from the Old Testament about the sure dangers of fraternization with secular, pagan standards of sexual behavior, marital fidelity, and family structure. In nearly every major Christian denomination—Lutheran, Methodist, Presbyterian, Episcopal, and Disciples of Christ—God's laws regarding marriage, divorce, sexuality, and gender differences are being discarded and replaced with corrupt human practices. Adultery and other sexual sins among religious leaders are at epidemic levels. In some denominations, divorce and remarriage among the clergy is hardly an issue. Some major Christian denominations have even begun to appoint practicing homosexuals as pastors, and a few have lesbian pastors.

When John the Baptist condemned the unlawful marriage of Herod Antipas and Herodias, he literally lost his head (Matthew

14:4-12). He would probably lose his head in many churches today, if he spoke against the clergy's unlawful divorces and remarriages. What do you think John would say about the popular no-fault-divorce churches or the nearly complete absence of moral courage among religious leaders when it comes to disciplining the scandalous marital and sexual behavior of many professing, church-going Christians?

THE NEED FOR EXEMPLARY CHURCH LEADERS

We must understand that the local church isn't a country club or a casual self-help group. It is God's holy temple, a congregation of redeemed saints and priests who are consecrated to God. It is God's lighthouse in a dark world. It is "the pillar and support of the truth." Thus Scripture commands: "But do not let immorality or any impurity or greed *even be named among you, as is proper among saints*" (Ephesians 5:3; italics added). In the classic work, *Studies in the Sermon on the Mount*, Martyn Lloyd-Jones writes:

> The glory of the gospel is that when the Church is absolutely different from the world, she invariably attracts it. It is then that the world is made to listen to her message, though it may hate it at first. That is how revival comes. That must also be true of us as individuals. It should not be our ambition to be as much like everybody else as we can, though we happen to be Christian, but rather to be as different from everybody who is not a Christian as we can possibly be. Our ambition should be to be like Christ, the more like Him the better, and the more like Him we become, the more we shall be unlike everybody who is not a Christian.[2]

I am absolutely convinced that a godly marriage lived according to God's laws is meant to be the means of untold blessing and is the best protection from the corrupting influences of this sinful world. It is certainly the very best protection and hope for our children and our churches. But a family can't stand alone in a morally degraded and hostile environment. So God, in His perfect wisdom, has given us a community of families—the local church—to help keep us pure from cultural defilement. The local church is perfectly designed to protect, support, and teach each Christian family.

Therefore Christian families need the local church. They need sound biblical teaching. They need to be shown God's wonderful design for the Christian home. They need to see good models of fatherhood and motherhood. They need to be under the disciplinary authority of the church. (See Matthew 18:17-20; 1 Corinthians 5; 2 Thessalonians 3:6-15; and Titus 3:10.)

A local church that is alive and functioning properly can help many families—perhaps even hundreds of families. Shepherds and deacons are chief among those who model God's design for the Christian home and provide sound teaching on Christian family life. This is one reason why God demands that their homes and marriages be in order.

A crucial step in Satan's strategy to destroy God's people is to destroy the marriages and families of those who lead the church. If he defiles the shepherds, the sheep will follow their sinful ways or be scattered. To protect the local church, God has placed specific marital and family qualifications for elders and deacons. Therefore, the church must insist that its leaders meet these qualifications before serving and while serving. If not, the local church will sink into the toxic wasteland of the world's marital and family values.

In marriage, child rearing, and general home management, deacons (and elders) must model God's design for faithful monogamous marriage and for a loving, disciplined, Christian household. In these fundamental areas of the Christian life, deacons must be above reproach. They must be "husbands of only one wife" and "good managers of their children and their own households." Let us examine these essential qualifications in depth.

FAMILY REQUIREMENTS FOR DEACONS

HUSBANDS OF ONLY ONE WIFE: FAITHFUL AND TRUE TO ONE WOMAN; A MAN WHOSE MARRIED LIFE EXEMPLIFIES GOD'S DESIGN OF FAITHFUL, MONAGAMOUS MARRIAGE

The phrase, "husbands of only one wife," and its related phrase, "the wife of one man," occur four times in the New Testament in the context of qualifications for either overseers, deacons, or widows. This phrase apparently expresses an exemplary Christian marital relationship, a husband-and-wife relationship that is above reproach. Here are its four occurrences.

• "An overseer, then, must be above reproach, the husband of one wife, temperate, prudent, respectable, hospitable, able to teach...." (1 Timothy 3:2).

• "Let deacons be husbands of only one wife, and good managers of their children and their own households" (1 Timothy 3:12).

• "Let a widow be put on the list only if she is not less than sixty years old, having been the wife of one man" (1 Timothy 5:9).

• "...if any man be above reproach, the husband of one wife, having children who believe, not accused of dissipation or rebellion" (Titus 1:6).

The phrase "husbands of only one wife" is made up of three words in Greek: *mias gynaikos andres:*

mias, one
gynaikos, wife/woman
andres, husbands/men

The words "one wife" are placed first in an emphatic position to stress the idea of "one wife." They modify the noun "husbands." We can translate this three-word phrase in the following ways: "one-wife husbands," "one-wife men," "one-woman men," or "husbands of one wife." (The word "only" is added by the translators of the *New American Standard Bible.*) However, there is broad disagreement on how to interpret this phrase, "husbands of only one wife." The following interpretations have been advanced.

Deacons Must Be Married

It's not uncommon for people to say that deacons (and overseers) must be married because Scripture says they must be the "husbands of only one wife." If Paul requires them to be married, however, he flatly contradicts what he teaches in 1 Corinthians 7 about the distinct advantages of singleness in serving the Lord. He boldly encourages singleness for more effective, undivided service to our Lord (1 Corinthians 7:32-35). So if deacons must be married, one must ask if his instruction on singleness is only for others, not for shepherds and deacons. If not, Paul should have qualified his statements about the advantage of singleness because singleness would disqualify an aspiring overseer or deacon. Paul didn't write, however, "Deacons must be men who have wives." He says that they must be *one-wife men,* which is quite a different point. Singleness does not disqualify a deacon.

A similar point is sometimes made regarding the qualification that deacons be "good managers of their children and their own houholds (3:12*b*)." Paul is not requiring a deacon to father two or more children. I've talked with men who don't believe they can serve as deacons or shepherds because they only have one child. They say that the qualification requires "children." But we must ask, "How else could Paul express himself?" He wouldn't use "child" because people would then think that deacons and elders were allowed to have only one child. We must not press Paul's words to absurd conclusions.

The fact is, most men are married and have children. Scripture requires that these men have their homes in order and that their marital relationships exemplify what Christian marriage should be. These qualifications don't apply to deacons who are single.

Deacons Are Prohibited from Polygamy

A number of biblical commentators believe that the phrase, "husbands of only one wife," means "married to one wife." They then conclude that Paul's intent was to prohibit polygamy—having two or more wives at the same time.

At first this may seem like a good explanation of this phrase, but the related phrase, "the wife of one man," makes it an almost impossible interpretation. In 1 Timothy 5:9, a widow qualifying for the widow's list must have been "the wife of one man." Certainly Paul wasn't thinking of women who had two or more husbands at one time, which is called polyandry. Polyandry was definitely not a problem in the church. Such a practice was abhorrent even to Jews and Romans. So it is most unlikely that the phrase, "husbands of only one wife," primarily addresses polygamy.

Deacons Must Be Married Only Once

Some prominent scholars and biblical commentators believe that this phrase means "married only once" and that no deacon can remarry. Paul, they believe, prohibits remarriage for any reason, even remarriage following the death of a spouse. Thus a widower who had remarried wouldn't qualify to be a deacon. If a deacon's wife dies, they believe, he can't remarry and remain a deacon.

This interpretation, however, is plainly at odds with the rest of the Bible's teaching on the sanctity of marriage.[3] "Nowhere else in the N.T.," writes J. E. Huther in *Meyer's Critical and Exegetical Handbook to the New Testament,* "is there the slightest trace of any ordinance against second marriages."[4]

By itself the phrase "husbands of only one wife" doesn't indicate whether each husband is to have one wife in an entire lifetime or one wife at a time. This phrase, therefore, must be interpreted in the larger context of Paul's overall teaching on marriage and must never be allowed to contradict God's clear, general teaching on marriage. It is highly questionable that this phrase is meant to disqualify remarried widowers. Therefore a remarried widower could still qualify to be called a "one-wife man."

Some commentators, however, apply this phrase only to remarriage after a divorce, not the death of a spouse. Among Jews, Romans, and Greeks, it was easy to divorce and remarry. In the case of remarriage after a divorce, unlike the death of a spouse, two or three living women could have been married to the same man. Some have termed this *successive polygamy*. They believe Paul prohibits a remarried divorcee from office because his ex-wife (or ex-wives) creates for the deacon, and the congregation, potentially offensive, embarrassing, or vulnerable situations. But if Paul specifically intended to prohibit divorced and remarried men from holding office, why didn't he say precisely that?

Deacons Must Be Faithful and True to One Woman

A final interpretation, and the one favored here, is that the phrase "husband of one wife" is meant to prohibit all sexual and marital deviation from faithful, monogamous marriages. This would prohibit deacons from polygamy, unlawful second marriages, concubinage, homosexuality, and/or any questionable relationship with the opposite sex. In English we would say, "The deacon is to be true to one woman" or "is to be a one-woman man," which, as you can see, closely follows the Greek wording.

A man may be, technically speaking, married to one woman, but have a girlfriend, or be flirtatious with other women, or consort with mistresses—a common practice among false teachers. So it is doubtful that Paul has in mind only the legal requirement of marriage to one spouse at one time and not the full intent of monogamous marriage.

Our Lord and Teacher, Jesus Christ, best explained God's design for marriage:

> "Have you not read, that He who created them from the beginning made them male and female, and said, 'For

this cause a man shall leave his father and mother, and shall cleave to his wife; and the two shall become one flesh'?

"Consequently they *are no longer two, but one flesh. What therefore God has joined together, let no man separate."* (Matthew 19:4*b*-6; italics added).

What kind of relationship does the candidate for office in the local church have with his wife and other women? Scripture answers that the candidate be a "one-wife" or "one-woman" man. A "one-woman man" has an exclusive relationship with one woman. He is above reproach in his sexual and marital life. He exemplifies faithful, monogamous marriage.

The phrase "husbands of only one wife" naturally raises agonizing questions that the phrase itself does not answer. For example, what about sexual and marital sins committed before a person's conversion to Christ? What about people who have legally divorced and remarried (assuming the local church allows for such)? What about the forgiveness and restoration of a fallen spiritual leader? These and many more questions must be answered from the whole of Scripture's teaching on divorce and remarriage, forgiveness, grace, restoration, and teaching on leadership example and qualification.

All marital deviations from God's standard confuse and perplex us. They raise painfully controversial questions. Sin always confuses, distorts, and divides, so there will always be diverse opinion on questions such as these. This in no way, however, diminishes the local church's obligation to face these issues and make wise, scripturally sound decisions. In all these heartbreaking situations, the honor of Jesus' name, faithfulness to His Word, and prayer are the supreme guides.

LET DEACONS BE . . . GOOD MANAGERS OF THEIR CHILDREN AND THEIR OWN HOUSEHOLDS

The emphasis in the text is on the word "good." In Greek, it is the adverb "well," "properly," or "excellently." So a candidate for the diaconate must supervise his family "well." This means he must be a responsible Christian father and household manager. He must provide for his family—financially, emotionally, and spiritually. His home must not be on the verge of collapse.

Having an orderly home means that the deacons' children (age not indicated) must obey and submit to his leadership in the home. (See 1 Timothy 3:4.) Yet he is not to be a spirit-crushing tyrant who gains submission by harsh punishment. The Bible implores the father to discipline and instruct his children, not provoke or exasperate them. Paul writes, "Fathers, do not provoke your children to anger; but bring them up in the discipline and instruction of the Lord" (Ephesians 6:4).

The Psalmist says, "Behold, children are a gift [heritage] of the Lord" (Psalm 127:3*a*). To lose this rich, eternal heritage is an incalculable loss. Quaker philosopher-theologian and church reformer, Elton Trueblood, places this matter in right perspective:

> No matter how much a man may be concerned with his work in the world, he cannot normally care about it as much as he cares for his family. This is because we have, in the life of the family, a bigger stake than most of us can ever have in our employment. We can change business associates...we can leave a poor job...but we cannot change *sons*. If we lose the struggle in our occupational interests, we can try again, but if we lose with our children our loss is terribly and frighteningly *final*.[5]

Also, the father must not be passive and disinterested in his children, the kind of man who leaves child rearing to his wife. He must actively guide and care for them and his entire household. As the Scripture says, "A child left to himself disgraces his mother" (Proverbs 29:15*b; New International Version*).

Children need constant training, discipline, and lots of love and affirmation. A Christian father must never be passive about the training of his children (Proverbs 3:12; 23:13,14; 29:17). If he is diligent, his children will benefit greatly and so will he. Solomon says, "A wise son makes a father glad (Proverbs 10:1*a*).

Scripture records the example of Job, a great father who should be an inspiration to all men who desire to serve God's family:

> And it came about, when the days of feasting had completed their cycle, that Job would send and consecrate them [his children], rising up early in the morning and offering burnt offerings according to the number of them all: for Job said, "Perhaps my sons have sinned and cursed God in their hearts." This Job did continually (Job 1:5).

Job acted as a priest on behalf of his children. He prayed for his children continually, and we can be sure that he taught them God's ways.

Please notice there are no perfect, problem-free children in this world. Even the best Christian fathers and mothers have child-related problems, but these parents resolve the problems and are involved with their children in responsible, caring ways. They guide their children through the many storms of life. Such fathers, who manage their children well, meet an important qualification for the diaconate.

The reason for this last qualification is obvious. A man's ability to manage God's church is directly related to his ability to manage his household. If he can't care for his family properly, he can't care for the family of God. In the family of God, a man's ability to manage his family is a crucial test as to whether or not he is qualified or disqualified to be a deacon.

Part Four

THE IMPORTANCE OF
DEACONS IN THE CHURCH

We are all too much occupied with taking care of ourselves; we shun the difficulties of excessive labour. And frequently behind the entrenchment of taking care of our constitution, we do not half as much as we ought. A minister of God is bound to spurn the suggestions of ignoble ease, it is his calling to labour; and if he destroys his constitution, I, for one, only thank God that he permits us the high privilege of so making ourselves living sacrifices.

Charles Haddon Spurgeon

Chapter 12

The Significance and Rewards of Deacons

> For those who have served well as deacons obtain for themselves a high standing and great confidence in the faith that is in Christ Jesus.
>
> **1 Timothy 3:13**

This final passage should be a source of enormous encouragement to deacons. Here Paul declares that faithful deacons gain significant influence and honor in the church, and that they can become spiritual powerhouses for God who exercise bold faith in Christ in all their labors. Let no one demean the church diaconate.

The little word "for" is important. It provides the logical connection between verse 13 and the preceding section (verses 8-12) and alerts us to why the requirements of verses 8 to 12 are necessary. Some people may question the high standards demanded of deacons since deacons are not on the same level as overseers. Verse 13, however, dispels any thought that deacons are insignificant or that their qualifications are not as necessary as those of overseers. At the same time, this verse provides encouragement and rich incentives for deacons to serve wholeheartedly.

DEACONS GAIN A PLACE OF INFLUENCE
AND HONOR IN THE CHURCH

What Paul says about deacons in verse 13 applies to deacons "who have served well." Only those who serve well—not necessarily those who are just on a church board—receive "a high standing." The word "well" indicates commendable service done in the right way. (See 1 Timothy 5:17.)

A deacon who serves well gains "a high standing," but what is this "high standing"? The Greek word for "standing," *bathmos*, means "a step," "a base of a pedestal," or "a stair." But the word is also used figuratively, as in verse 13, to mean "position," "standing," or a "grade of advancement."

A few commentators believe that the phrase "high standing" means "an advance in rank." Therefore, they assume that the reward for good service is a promotion to the higher office of eldership. This view, however, is built on false notions of the diaconate. Some deacons who serve excellently will never qualify to be pastor-elders because they are not able to teach. Deacons do not have to be able to teach, but elders do. The diaconate, therefore, is not a steppingstone to the eldership.

Furthermore, the word "high" is the Greek word *kalos,* which means "good." Paul says that the faithful deacon gains "a good standing," not a better standing. Paul is not saying that the eldership is good and that the diaconate is not good. Such ideas contradict the purpose of verse 13, which is to encourage deacons.

Other scholars suggest that Paul's statement is a reference to the deacons' standing at the judgment seat of Christ. Deacons, they claim, will obtain an excellent position in glory. Still others say that "high standing" is a higher stage of spiritual life. These interpretations, however, seem farfetched and out of context.

Paul uses *bathmos* in this context to mean a "standing" or, as Hunter says, "a degree of honor."[1] E. K. Simpson, a renowned scholar of Hellenistic Greek literature, writes, "We should translate it *an honourable standing*."[2] Hort renders the thought this way: "an excellent vantage ground."[3] The word "high" in Greek, *kalos,* means "good," "noble," or "praiseworthy." Verse 13, then, communicates the idea that *a faithful, diligent deacon can gain for himself a place of influence and honor.*

From the context, we can assume that the primary source of this standing of influence and honor is the Christian community. Of course, if a deacon gains a good standing in the local church, he would also have such a standing before God. However, the good standing Paul is describing relates more directly to the sphere in which the deacons' service is performed, not the deacons' standing in eternity.

Everything Paul writes in this verse about deacons relates to their serving others well (verse 13*a).* The point of this entire section (3:8-12) is to convey the deacons' qualifications and to emphasize the importance of their examination before the local church. Deacons must be found to be above reproach by their brothers and sisters before they can serve in an official capacity. Verse 13 reinforces, for both the deacons and the congregation, the necessity for the qualifications. Precisely because deacons can acquire such a place of honor, deacon candidates must be properly qualified and tested before they serve.

Furthermore, verse 13 is parallel to 1 Timothy 3:1, where Paul writes a similar statement about overseers. He encourages men to serve as overseers by saying, "If any man aspires to the office of overseer, it is a fine work [good task] he desires to do" (verse 1). Perhaps Paul senses that a positive and encouraging statement is also needed concerning deacons. The people may have overlooked and underestimated the deacons. So Paul assures his readers that deacons also do a good work and thus can gain for themselves esteem and influence in the church.

What a tremendous privilege it is to have an honorable standing in God's house! It is better than having a good standing in the highest government position or in a prestigious university. God's household—His church—is the most important institution on earth.

I'd like to share a contemporary illustration that communicates Paul's thought in verse 13. Once a year, a survey is taken to choose the ten most-respected people in the world. Interestingly few, glittering movie stars or wealthy people are chosen. Every year, the Roman Catholic nun, Mother Teresa, tops the list. For more than forty years, she has poured herself out to serve the poorest of the poor in Calcutta, India. Today she is one of the world's most highly regarded and influential women. Deacons who serve people well will, in a similar way, gain a place of honor and influence.

DEACONS GAIN GREAT BOLDNESS IN FAITH

Not only do deacons who serve well gain a good standing and reputation in the church, they also gain "great confidence in the faith that is in Christ Jesus." Let us look closely at this second reward for diligent service.

The word "confidence" (Greek, *parrēsia*) is an important New Testament word that can mean "open, free speech." Thus a number of translators believe that Paul is referring to the deacons' confidence in speaking openly about the faith. The *New English Bible* reads, "For deacons with a good record of service may claim a high standing and the right to speak openly on matters of the Christian faith." This translation, however, seems out of place within this context on the deacons' work.

In the New Testament, "confidence" most often means "openness," "firm confidence," or "boldness" in a general sense, without reference to speech. It is the opposite of reserve, fear, concealment, or timidity. In the present passage, "confidence" is an acceptable but weak translation. Boldness, as rendered in the *Authorized Version,* is better and fits with the prepositional phrase that follows: "in the faith."

Paul is saying that these deacons will gain much boldness in their faith in Christ. The deacons' boldness is specifically in the area of "the faith," or, as the original Greek says, "in faith." In verse 13, "faith" does not refer to a fixed set of doctrines but to the deacons' personal, experiential faith centered in Christ. (This type of subjective faith is mentioned in 1 Timothy 1:4,5,14,19; 2:15; 6:12.)

We might think that because deacons serve people's physical welfare, they would not need to acquire boldness in faith. But such is not the case. Their work demands spiritual power and faith. Deacons need spiritual vitality and life. Do not underestimate the potential influence the diaconate can have on the local church.

Deacons can do mighty deeds for God and His people. They can expand their ministry in many ways. They can profoundly influence the congregation. They can be living examples of Christlike compassion and mercy. Furthermore, diligent deacons gain for themselves not just boldness in faith, but *much* boldness in faith. What better virtue can a deacon gain than *much boldness in faith,* which enhances his work enormously.

The word "faith" is one of the most significant words in the New Testament. In its noun, verb, and adjectival forms, "faith" occurs more than 307 times in the New Testament. In the words of Nigel Turner, faith "is indeed the Christian life.... It is the channel which conveys a saint's distinctive blessings, peace with God, hope, joy, forgiveness and salvation. From it, all the graces spring to adorn the life of the Christian fellowship."[4]

Our faith is a dynamic quality. It can grow strong and increase (2 Thessalonians 1:3; 2 Corinthians 10:15), or it can become weak. It can endure, or it can fail. It is always under attack. Satan seeks to destroy our faith because it is the key to resisting him and winning in spiritual warfare (Ephesians 6:16; 1 Peter 5:8,9; 1 John 5:4; 1 Thessalonians 5:8). Faith affects our prayers. Faith governs the exercise of our spiritual gifts (Romans 12:3,6). Faith motivates us to greater love and service (2 Thessalonians 1:11).

The whole Christian life is to be marked by faith—"trust" in Christ. The wonderful thing we learn from 1 Timothy 3:13 is that as deacons faithfully serve, they also develop their spiritual lives, particularly their faith in Christ. Although deacons do not teach or govern the congregation, they can be spiritual giants who exercise bold faith. Those who are bold in faith venture out into new faith-inspired works for God. This bold faith will result in their doing greater exploits for God, in moving mountains, in generating creative new ideas for showing mercy and Christ's love to others, in gaining new vision, and in going beyond minimal duties. As deacons serve well, they gain boldness in their faith to do even more. Men of faith are men of action and deeds.

Faith cannot deepen and grow without resistance from trials and labors. Christian apologist, Os Guinness, likens the strengthening of faith to an athlete's bodily training:

> Like a sportsman in training, faith must keep itself fit. It must be trim and in good shape. It must keep its hand in and never be out of practice. It will have its limits, but it will know them and do its best to extend them. What it fears above all is the test which shows that its training has gone to seed, its muscles have grown soft, its confidence has been misplaced.... Not surprisingly, many of the biblical pictures of faith are strenuous, active and energetic. Faith is the athlete straining for the finishing line, the boxer kept in superb condition by his training, the soldier stripped to his essential equipment.... Faith presses forward or is pushed back. Faith trains or grows slack.[5]

Unbelief, on the other hand, paralyzes men. It halts action. It destroys vision. It creates disobedience and discouragement. Listen to Moses' words concerning Israel's unbelief: "And when the Lord sent you from Kadesh-barnea, saying, 'Go up and possess the land which I have given you,' then you rebelled against the command of the Lord your God; you neither believed Him nor listened to His voice" (Deuteronomy 9:23).

Notice that the faith Paul describes in 1 Timothy 3:13 is not rooted in the deacons' own intelligence, skill, energy, or financial resources. This faith is rooted "in Christ Jesus." Biblical faith points to Christ, not to self. It is Christ-centered faith, and the object of our faith makes all the difference. It is faith in the One who empowers and sustains us. It is faith in the anointed Son of God, Jesus Christ our Savior.

Except for a few references to God, nearly all the New

Testament references establish Jesus Christ as the supreme object of our faith. He leads us to the Father. We can only know God through Christ. Without Christ, we cannot approach or serve God. Without Him, we can do nothing (John 15:5).

Our faith determines our capacity for God's service. For example, when the disciples asked why they had failed to cure a demon-possessed young man, Jesus said that their failure was due to their lack of faith:

> And He said to them, "Because of the littleness of your faith; for truly I say to you, if you have faith as a mustard seed, you shall say to this mountain, 'Move from here to there,' and it shall move; and nothing shall be impossible to you'" (Matthew 17:20; cf. 1 Corinthians 13:2).

All that we truly do for God is done according to our faith. The writer of Hebrews illustrates the power of faith at work through the Old Testament heroes of faith "who by faith conquered kingdoms, performed acts of righteousness, obtained promises, shut the mouths of lions, quenched the power of fire, escaped the edge of the sword, from weakness were made strong, became mighty in war, put foreign armies to flight" (Hebrew 11:33,34). Luke, also, refers to Stephen, one of the Seven, as "a man full of faith" (Acts 6:5).

To acquire great boldness in faith is to gain a tremendous prize! Could deacons gain anything better than boldness in faith in Christ? What a wonderful prize. What a wonderful ministry deacons can accomplish.

Chapter 13

Agents of Christ's Mercy

"Be merciful, just as your Father is merciful"
Luke 6:36

If you have the gift of showing mercy, do it cheerfully
Romans 12:8d *The New Translation*

Among the many profound words of the Bible, the word *mercy* stands out as the word that communicates hope and comfort. In a world plagued by suffering and sin, we continually need mercy from God and our fellow man. For a simple definition of mercy, Lawrence O. Richards writes, "In both Testaments, mercy is compassion expressed to meet human need."[1] Carl Armerding, writing in *The Zondervan Encyclopedia of the Bible*, gives a fuller definition of mercy:

> ...a disposition to spare or help another. This disposition, although inwardly felt, manifests itself outwardly in some

kind of action. It is evident that mercy combines a strong emotional element, usually identified as pity, compassion, or love, with some practical demonstration of kindness in response to the condition or needs of the object of mercy.[2]

In his book, *Ministries of Mercy,* Timothy J. Keller remarks, "'Mercy' is the impulse that makes us sensitive to hurts and lacks in others and makes us desire to alleviate them."[3] Quoting a Puritan writer, Keller also says, "'Grace has to do with man's merits, but *mercy* has to do with man's misery.'"[4]

The Bible teaches that God is full of mercy. The prophet Jeremiah cries out, "It is of the Lord's mercies that we are not consumed" (Lamentations 3:22a; *Authorized Version*). If it were not for God's mercy toward needy, unworthy sinners, we would all be lost in our sins. Indeed Scripture says, "But God, being rich in mercy,...even when we were dead in our transgressions, made us alive together with Christ" (Ephesians 2:4a,5a).

Our Lord, as He walked this earth, did much to relieve the human misery of those around Him. To a raving, demon-filled man whom He healed, He said, "'Go home to your people and report to them what great things the Lord has done for you, and how *He had mercy on you*'" (Mark 5:19; italics added).

The marvelous story of the Good Samaritan is a touching and instructive illustration of human mercy in action (Luke 10:30-37). When the Samaritan found a nearly dead, beaten, stripped, and robbed man on the road to Jericho, the Bible says "he felt compassion" for him. Deeply stirred in his soul by the plight of the helpless man, the Samaritan took immediate action to relieve his suffering. He "bandaged up his wounds, pouring oil and wine on them; and he put him on his own beast, and brought him to an inn, and took care of him." The following day the Samaritan told the innkeeper "'Take care of him; and whatever more you spend, when I return, I will repay you.'"

An inquiring lawyer called what the Samaritan did for this suffering man "showing mercy" (Luke 10:37). Concurring with this lawyer's analysis, Jesus added, "'Go and do the same.'"

DEACONS ARE THE AGENTS OF MERCY
IN CHRIST'S CHURCH

Deacons, as we've seen, are to serve the felt needs of people. Their task is best described in Acts 6 by the twelve apostles:

> "It is not desirable for us [the church overseers] to neglect the word of God in order to serve tables [collect and administer funds for the poor]. But select from among you, brethren, seven men...whom we may put in charge of *this task* [poor relief]" (Acts 6:2,3; italics added).

Through the deacons, the local church's charitable activities are effectively organized and centralized. The deacons are collectors of funds, distributors of relief, and agents of mercy. They help the poor, the jobless, the sick, the widowed, the elderly, the homeless, the shut-in, the refugees, and the disabled. They counsel and guide people. They visit people in their homes. They relieve suffering. They comfort, protect, and encourage people, and help to meet their needs. In contemporary language, they are the congregation's social workers.

Their work, though often hard and exasperating, is most precious in God's eyes. He is deeply concerned about the poor and needy. "This is pure and undefiled religion...," declares James, "to visit orphans and widows in their distress..." (James 1:27). Caring for the needy is essential business in authentic Christianity. Yet, the needy are often neglected and even despised. This should not be! The local church must care for its needy members, and the diaconate is the official church body responsible for this task.

In the New Testament, deacons are always in close relationship with the shepherds of the church. Like the shepherds, they are required to meet specific qualifications. Like the shepherds, they must be officially examined and approved before they can serve. Like the shepherds, they hold an official position of trust in the congregation. Unlike the shepherds of the church, however, deacons do not teach or govern as part of their position. They are servant-officers who relieve shepherds of the multitude of practical duties that are required in caring for a congregation. The two offices of overseer and deacon are separate but complementary. The shepherd-elders must give their primary attention to teaching and leading the people. Deacons must give their primary attention to caring for the people's physical welfare. Tragically, however, many church deacons are uncertain about who they are and what they are to do. So they suffer, shepherds suffer, congregations suffer, and those who need their care suffer the most.

Among Bible-believing churches, two extremes continually threaten the New Testament diaconate. The first is to make deacons the power brokers and rulers of the church. In many churches, deacons form the chief executive board. This practice blatantly ignores all New Testament facts about deacons and completely distorts the New Testament diaconate.

The other extreme demeans deacons to nearly janitor status. But the New Testament diaconate was never intended to be a building-maintenance committee. If your congregation owns a building, form a building-maintenance committee. The people on that committee do not need to meet God's qualifications for deaconship, nor do they need to be publicly examined and approved. If you need a deacon on the committee to facilitate good church management and communication, that is acceptable, but do not allow the diaconate to lose its primary focus, which inevitably happens when it assumes sole responsibility for the church building.

We must not forget that the real treasures of the church are its people, not its pews and buildings. Yet, so often the needy are left unattended, and the church building receives priority attention both in time and funds.

The deacons hold a distinct office of loving service to those who are in distress, to those who are dear to God's heart. As is so admirably illustrated for us in Acts 6, the deacons' office is essential to the local church and our witness for Christ. Deacons have the honor of modeling, for the local church and a lost world, God's compassion, kindness, mercy, and love. When the local church compassionately cares for peoples' needs, the world sees a visible display of Christ's love, which will draw some people to the Savior. So every local church needs faithful, dedicated deacons who have Christ's compassionate heart for the needy.

DEACONS ARE TO MODEL THEMSELVES AFTER JESUS

When our merciful Lord came to this self-centered, self-seeking, prideful world, the virtues of humility and servanthood received radically new meaning and significance (Matthew 20:20-28; Luke 12:37). So if we want to truly understand the Christian idea of servanthood or service, we should study Christ's life, which is a story of loving, selfless "service" to others. He was a servant *par excellence*. The following few Scriptures tell of Christ's loving *diakonia:*

• "And they were utterly astonished, saying, 'He has done all things well; He makes even the deaf to hear, and the dumb to speak'" (Mark 7:37).

• "'You know of Jesus of Nazareth,...how He went about doing good, and healing all who were oppressed by the devil; for God was with Him'" (Acts 10:38).

• "And the blind and the lame came to Him in the temple, and He healed them. But when the chief priests and the scribes *saw the wonderful things that He had done*...they became indignant..." (Matthew 21:14,15; italics added).

• "And moved with compassion, Jesus touched their eyes; and immediately they regained their sight and followed Him" (Matthew 20:34).

• "And Jesus was going about all the cities...proclaiming the gospel of the kingdom, and healing every kind of disease and every kind of sickness. And seeing the multitudes, He felt compassion for them, because they were distressed and downcast like sheep without a shepherd" (Matthew 9:35,36).

• "And Jesus answered and said to them, 'Go and report to John what you hear and see: the blind receive sight and the lame walk, the lepers are cleansed and the deaf hear, and the dead are raised up, and the poor have the gospel preached to them'" (Matthew 11:4,5).

As servant-officers, deacons are to have their true identity in Jesus Christ. Jesus Christ is to be their model and example. They are to be distinctly Christian servants—loving, sacrificial, willing, compassionate, and merciful. May all Christian deacons be blessed as they seek to imitate Christ's compassionate, unselfish concern for those in distress. May they be like Him as they serve in this esteemed office.

NOTES

Facing the Issues

1. For over a thousand years the Roman Catholic Church relegated
   the position of deacon to an apprenticeship to the priesthood.
   The diaconate was an ordained position in the clerical hierarchy,
   but it was only a transitional step to the higher order of priesthood. Its significance was largely ceremonial.

   Today, however, among Catholics there is widespread
   deacon renewal. In America and Germany the Roman Catholic
   diaconal ministry is flourishing with thousands of men involved.
   In 1963, at Vatican II, a provision was made for the restoration of
   the "permanent deacon," both celibate and married. The historic
   decision on deacons at Vatican II reads: "At a lower level of the
   hierarchy are deacons, upon whom hands are imposed 'not unto
   the priesthood, but unto a ministry of service.'...they serve the
   People of God in the ministry of the liturgy, of the word, and of
   charity" (*Lumen Gentium* 29, trans. by Mgr. Joseph Gallagher in
   Walter M. Abbott, ed., *The Documents of Vatican II* [New York:
   Guild Press, 1966], p. 55). Under the bishop's direction, these
   deacons involve themselves with liturgical, teaching, pastoral,
   and charitable duties.

   The Anglican Communion has also historically relegated the
   diaconate to an apprenticeship to the priesthood, "an apprenticeship," as one theologian says, "to be discharged as quickly as
   possible" (Edmond LaB. d'Etre, "The Order of Deacons inAngli-
   canism: A Deacon's 'Raison d'Etre," in *The Diaconate Now*, ed.
   Richard T. Nolan [Washington: Corpus Books, 1968], p.116).

   The Episcopal Church in America, however, has moved
   ahead with what it calls the "perpetual diaconate." These
   deacons are nonsalaried or salaried men and women who are
   trained and ordained to a vocational diaconate. They are an
   official part of the clergy, and they perform a wide variety of
   services— liturgical, administrative, pastoral, and charitable—
   both within the church and without.

   In the Eastern Orthodox Church the diaconate has been
   primarily liturgical and administrative in nature. Charitable and
   social services are performed by the laity or other institutions, not
   by deacons. With the extreme shortage of priests, most men out
   of seminary remain deacons only a few weeks or months before

they move on to the priesthood. In most places the permanent diaconate is disappearing. So there is little interest in diaconate renewal.

Interest for renewal or recovery of the diaconate among Presbyterians, Baptists, Assemblies of God, the Reformed, and Methodists is witnessed by the following books: Joan S. Gray and Joyce C. Tucker, *Presbyterian Polity for Church Officers,* (Atlanta: John Knox Press 1986), pp. 44-55. Charles W. Deweese, *The Emerging Role of Deacons* (Nashville: Broadman Press, 1979); Richard L. Dresselhaus, *The Deacon and His Ministry* (Springfield: Gospel Publishing House, 1977); Elsie Anne McKee, *DIAKONIA in the Classical Reformed Tradition and Today* (Grand Rapids: William B. Eerdmans Publishing Company, 1989); Rosemary Skinner Keller, Gerald F. Moede, and Mary Elizabeth Moore, *Called to Serve: The United Methodist Diaconate.*

2. Rosemary Skinner Keller, Gerald F. Moede, and Mary Elizabeth Moore, *Called to Serve: The United Methodist Diaconate* (Nashville: UMC General Board of Higher Education and Ministry, 1987), p. 2.

3. Richard L. Dresselhaus, *The Deacon and His Ministry* (Springfield: Gospel Publishing House, 1977), p. 10.

4. Ibid, pp. 43,44.

5. Charles W. Deweese, *The Emerging Role of Deacons* (Nashville: Broadman Press, 1979), p. 62.

6. By the middle of the third century the deacon emerged as the liturgical and executive assistant of the bishop. He became a predominant and powerful figure in the church. In one of the early church order manuals called, *Apostolic Tradition,* Hippolytus, writing from Rome about A.D. 215 states:

> In the ordination of a deacon, the bishop alone shall lay on hands, because he is not being ordained to the priesthood, but to the service of the bishop, to do what is ordered by him. For he does not share in the counsel of the presbyterate, but administers and informs the bishop of what is fitting (Geoffrey J. Cuming, *Hippolytus: A Text for Students* [Bramcote Notts: Grove Books, 1976], p. 13).

The deacon became the bishop's representative, liaison man, and reporter. He was administrator, pastoral assistant, and charity worker. He was, in the words of another church order manual, "the bishop's ear, and eye, and mouth, and heart, and soul ("Constitutions of the Holy Apostles," in *The Ante-Nicene Fathers*, 10 vols., eds Alexander Roberts and James Donaldson [repr. Grand Rapids: William B. Eerdmans Publishing Company, n.d.], 7:416).

In some cases, because of his close association with the bishop, the deacon succeeded the bishop in his office. One notable example is Athanasius, the great defender of the faith against Arianism. He was a deacon and assistant to Alexander, the bishop of Alexandria. When the bishop died (A.D. 328), Athanasius became his successor.

With such prominence it was inevitable that deacons would at times tower over presbyters (elders). "In the third century," writes Dr. James M. Barnett, an Episcopalian scholar, "the deacons seem often to have overshadowed the presbyters in their importance and influence" (*The Diaconate, A Full and Equal Order* [New York: Seabury Press, 1981], p. 67). Ambrosiaster, who wrote *On the Boastfulness of the Roman Deacons,* and Jerome complained of the excessive prestige and power of some deacons. Jerome (c. A.D. 345-419) wrote a letter to a man named Evangelus refuting those who had made deacons greater than presbyters: "I am told that someone has been mad enough to put deacons before presbyters, that is, before bishops [Jerome knew that presbyters and bishops were originally the same]" ("Letters," in *Nicene and Post-Nicene Fathers*, 14 vols., Second Series, eds. Philip Schaff and Henry Wace [repr. Grand Rapids: William B. Eerdmans Publishing Company, n.d.] 6:288).

Also at the council of Nicaea in A.D. 325, the bishops addressed what they considered the overreaching activities of some deacons. Canon eighteen states: "let the deacons remain within their own bounds, knowing that they are the ministers of the bishop and the inferiors of the presbyters.... And if, after this decree, any one shall refuse to obey, let him be deposed from the diaconate" ("The Seven Ecumenical Councils," in *Nicene and Post-Nicene Fathers,* Second Series, 14:38). But this "Golden Age" of the deacon (A.D. 100-600), as it is sometimes called, eventually deteriorated in the West. A number of factors led to its decline:

(1) The requirement that deacons be celibate.

(2) The change in the bishop's role from local pastor to supervisor over many churches. This placed new duties and powers into the hands of the local presbyter (priest), duties that deacons once performed.

(3) The lack of clear definition of the deacon's role and status. Because of this and the previous point, the deacon's role gradually narrowed to include mainly liturgical functions. The deacon's main duties centered around the altar.

Catholic scholar, Joseph W. Pokusa writes, "The evidence of canonical texts from the time of Isidore of Seville through the age of Gratian emphasizes that most deacons had come to exercise a nearly exclusively liturgical ministry...a purely liturgical diaconate had become a thoroughly accepted idea. Whatever other occupations were peculiar to exceptional, individual deacons, in practice and in theory the Church asked of clerics in the diaconal grade simply subordinate liturgical service" (*A Canonical-Historical Study of the Diaconate in the Western Church* [Washington: The Catholic University of America, 1979], p. 208).

(4) The ordered succession of clerical grades from lower to higher—minor orders, deacon, priest, bishop—made the diaconate less desirable to men. Thus the diaconate became a token office, a preparatory stage for the priesthood.

7. Among the reformers, at the time of the mighty sixteenth-century reformation, John Calvin made the most conscientious effort to restore the New Testament deacon. This book is basically in agreement with Calvin's sixteenth-century reform of the church diaconate. See John Calvin, *The Institutes of the Christian Religion*, 2 vols., trans. F.L. Battles, ed. J.T. McNeill [Philadelphia: Westminster Press, 1960], 2:1061,1062,1097,1098.

8. Jonathan Edwards, *The Works of Jonathan Edwards,* 2 vols. (1834; repr. Edinburgh: The Banner of Truth Trust, 1974), 2:164.

9. In a commentary on its own pronouncement on deacons, the Faith and Order Commission of the World Council of Churches states: "In many churches there is today considerable uncertainty about the need, the rationale, the status and the functions of deacons" (*Baptism, Eucharist and Ministry,* Faith and Order Paper 111 [Geneva: World Council of Churches, 1982], comment on M. 31, p. 27).

Chapter 1: The Shepherds' Priorities

1. John Owen, "Of Deacons," in *The Works of John Owen,* 16 vols., ed. William H. Goold (London: Johnstone and Hunter, 1850-53; repr. Edinburgh: The Banner of Truth Trust, 1968), 16:145.

NOTES

2. Richard N. Longenecker, "Acts," in *The Expositor's Bible Commentary,* 12 vols., ed. Frank E. Gaebelein (Grand Rapids: Zondervan Publishing House, 1981), 9:289.
3. Robert and Julia Banks, *The Home Church* (Sutherland: Albatross Books, 1986), p. 82.
4. Paul E. Billheimer, *Destined for the Throne* (Fort Washington, PA: Christian Literature Crusade, 1975), pp. 101,102,104.
5. D. Martyn Lloyd-Jones, *Preaching and Preachers* (Grand Rapids: Zondervan Publishing House, 1971), p. 23.
6. Ibid., pp. 24, 25.
7. J.I. Packer, "Why Preach," in *The Preacher and Preaching,* ed. Samuel T. Logan (Phillipsburg: Presbyterian and Reformed Publishing Company, 1986), p. 3.
8. John R.W. Stott, *Between Two Worlds: The Art of Preaching in the Twentieth Century* (Grand Rapids: William B. Eerdmans Publishing Company, 1982), p. 206.
9. Ibid., p. 124.

Chapter 2: Appointing Ministers of Mercy

1. John Calvin, *The Acts of the Apostles,* 2 vols., trans. J. W. Fraser and W. J. G. Mc Donald, ed. D. W. and T. F. Torrance (Grand Rapids: William B. Eerdmans Publishing Company, 1965), 1:130.
2. Benjamin Breckinridge Warfield, "The Emotional Life of Our Lord," in *The Person and Work of Christ* (Philadelphia: The Presbyterian and Reformed Publishing Company, 1950), p. 104.
3. D. Martyn Lloyd-Jones, *Studies in the Sermon on the Mount,* 2 vols. (Grand Rapids: William B. Eerdmans Publishing Company, 1971), 2:94.
4. Quoted by Ronald J. Sider in *Rich Christians in an Age of Hunger* (Downers Grove: InterVarsity Press, 1984), p. 109.
5. "Waste in government worse than ever, Congress is told" in the *Rocky Mountain News,* Nov. 29, 1989.
6. Joachim Jeremias, *Jerusalem in the Time of Jesus* (Philadelphia: Fortress Press, 1969), pp. 126-134.

Chapter 3: Official Public Recognition

1. The subject of the Greek participle for "praying" and the Greek verb that means "laid their hands on" is a bit ambiguous. Grammatically, we might expect the congregation to be the subject of all the verbs in Acts 6:6. But the context as a whole, especially

verse 3, favors the apostles as the subject of "praying" and "laid their hands on them."

2. R.J. Knowling, "The Acts of the Apostles," in *The Expositor's Greek Testament,* 5 vols., ed. W. Robertson Nicoll (1900-10; repr. Grand Rapids: William B. Eerdmans Publishing Company, 1976), 2:169.

3. James Orr, "Hands, Imposition of," in *The International Standard Bible Encyclopedia,* 5 vols., ed. James Orr (1929; repr. Grand Rapids: William B. Eerdmans Publishing Company, 1955) 2:1335.

4. Robert Murray McCheyne, "Sermon 82," in *The Works of Robert Murray McCheyne,* ed. Andrew A. Bonar (New York: Robert Carter and Brothers, 1883), 2:482.

5. John Owen, "Of Deacons," in *The Works of John Owen,* 16 vols., ed. W. H.Goold (London: Johnstone and Hunter, 1850-53; repr. Edinburgh: Banner of Truth Trust, 1968), 16:144.

6. Ibid., p. 144.

7. Ibid., p. 144.

8. William Barclay, *The Gospel of Matthew,* 2 vols. (Philadelphia: The Westminster Press, 1958), 1:244.

Chapter 4: Acts 6: The Prototype

1. Irenaeus, "Against Heresies," in *The Ante-Nicene Fathers,* 10 vols., eds. Alexander Roberts and James Donaldson (Edinburgh: T.&T. Clark, n.d.; repr. Grand Rapids: William B. Eerdmans Publishing Company, 1989), 1:434. (Hereafter cited as *The Ante-Nicene Fathers.*)

2. Gordon Fee, *1 and 2 Timothy, Titus,* New International Biblical Commentary (Peabody: Hendrickson Publishers, 1988), p. 86.

3. F.F. Bruce, *The Acts of the Apostles: Greek Text with Introduction and Commentary,* (3rd. ed., Grand Rapids: William B. Eerdmans Publishing Company, 1990), p. 27.

4. Ibid., p. 18.

5. Bruce claims that, "Nowhere in Acts is Paul called 'apostle' in the special sense in which he uses the designation of himself in his letters" (*The Acts of the Apostles,* p. 319).

6. William Ramsay, *St. Paul the Traveller and the Roman Citizen* (London: Hodder and Stoughton, 1897; repr. Grand Rapids: Baker Book House, 1962), pp. 20,21.

7. David Gooding, *True to the Faith, A Fresh Approach to the Acts of the Apostles* (London: Hodder and Stoughton, 1990), p. 426.

8. *Diakonia* with the meaning, "service to the needy": Acts 11:29; 12:25; Romans 15:31; 2 Corinthians 8:4; 9:1,12,13.

NOTES

Diakoneō: Matthew 25:44; Romans 15:25; Hebrews 6:10; 2 Corinthians 8:19,20.

9. C.E.B. Cranfield, "Diakonia in the New Testament," in *Service in Christ: Essays Presented to Karl Barth on his 80th Birthday,* ed. J.I. McCord and T.H.L. Parker (Grand Rapids: William B. Eerdmans Publishing Company, 1966), p. 39.

10. F.F. Bruce, *The Book of the Acts,* The New International Commentary on the New Testament (rev. ed., Grand Rapids: William B. Eerdmans Publishing Company, 1988), p. 3.

11. Hermann W. Beyer, *"diakonos,"* in *Theological Dictionary of the New Testament,* eds. G. Kittel and G. Friedrich, trans. and ed. G.W. Bromiley, 10 vols. (Grand Rapids: William B. Eerdmans Publishing Company, 1964-76), 2 (1964): 90. (Hereafter cited as *Theological Dictionary of the New Testament.*)

12. Michael Green, *Called To Serve: Ministry and Ministers in the Church,* in the series "Christian Foundations" (Philadelphia: The Westminster Press, 1964), p. 52.

13. A few writers have suggested that Acts 6 is the account of the origin of the first Christian elders. They think this because in Acts 11:30 the financial contribution from Antioch to the poor in Jerusalem was handed over to the elders, not the Seven or deacons. But this is a far fetched idea. The elders received the offering from Antioch because they were the leaders of the church. And one of their functions as the official representative body of the church was to receive all official communications from other churches (Acts 15:2; 21:17,18). The money received by the elders was a gift from outside their congregation, not from within. Moreover, Luke does not say they distributed the funds to the needy. Others most likely would do that.

Luke does not need to tell of the origin of the eldership, it is one of the oldest, best established institutions of the Old Testament.

14. James Monroe Barnett, *The Diaconate, A Full and Equal Order* (New York: Seabury Press, 1981), p. 30.

15. F. J. A. Hort, *The Christian Ecclesia* (London: Macmillan and Company, 1914), p. 209.

Chapter 5: Overseers

1. H. W. Beyer, *"episkopos,"* in *Theological Dictionary of the New Testament,* 2(1964):612.

2. Ibid., p. 614.

3. Some commentators believe that the terms *overseers* and *deacons* are used functionally to designate all the people in the church

166

who supervise and serve the local church. They support this view by the absence of the definite article before the terms *overseers* and *deacons*. But the absence of the definite article in Greek is insufficient reason to assign a purely functional sense to these terms for the following reasons:

(1) The context itself makes the terms definite. After addressing all the saints, Paul makes special mention to two distinct groups. If Paul wanted to speak generally, he would not have used the noun forms as he did. He would have most likely used the participial forms *overseeing* and *serving*.

H.C.G. Moule writes, "Context in a case like this sufficiently defines; the persons of the classes named are self- evidently those at Philippi" (*The Epistle to the Philippians,* Cambridge Greek Testament for Schools and Colleges [Cambridge: The University Press, 1897], p. 12).

(2) The nouns *episkopos* and, to a lesser extent, *diakonos* were recognized, official designations in Greek society. Former professor of Biblical criticism at the University of Glasgow, Ernest Best writes:

> I say "officials" because *episkopos* at any rate could not have been used in any other way than as a designation of an office.... A first century Greek could not have used it in a purely functional sense without suggesting that the person who exercised oversight held "official" status. There is also some, though less, evidence that *diakonos* was used in the same way. The fact that one was certainly used in the sense of a group of officials implies that the other was also ("Bishops and Deacons: Philippians 1:1," in *Studia Evangelica*, ed. F.L.Cross [Berlin: Akademia Verlag, 1968] 4:371).

(3) There is obvious similarity between the joint use of the words "overseers" and "deacons" in this passage and those found in 1 Timothy 3:1-13. Both letters were written in the early to mid sixties. We know there were overseers and deacons at Ephesus during this time, so likely there were also officially recognized overseers and deacons at Philippi.

The interpretation, then, that assigns only a functional meaning to the words *overseers* and *deacons* is confusing and nearly meaningless.

4. The Greek word for "elder" is *presbyteros,* which is derived from the adjective *presbys,* which means "old." *Presbyteros* is the comparative form, meaning "older" (Luke 15:25). However, in many cases the comparative force disappears and it simply means "old" or "old man." The problem with *presbyteros* is its two-fold meaning. It can mean:

(1) "older man" or "old man," as in 1 Timothy 5:1: "Do not sharply rebuke an older man [*presbyteros*]."

(2) a title for a community official, a ruler, or an "elder," as in 1 Timothy 5:17: "Let the elders [*presbyteroi*] who rule well be considered worthy of double honor...."

In a few contexts it is hard to know which of these is meant. However, most of the time it is clear which meaning is intended.

5. Polycarp, *Philippians,* 5. (All quotes from the early Apostolic Fathers are taken from J.B. Lightfoot's and R.J. Harmer's *The Apostolic Fathers,* (London: Macmillan and Company, 1891; repr. Grand Rapids: Baker Book House, 1984.)

6. Philippians 1:1 states that the church had a plurality of overseers as well as deacons. Thus a team of overseers jointly pastored the congregation. To claim, as some do, that there were several congregations in Philippi, each having a single overseer, is pure guesswork. It is also a gross misunderstanding of the elder-system of government. Philippians 4:15, and especially Polycarp's letter to the Philippians, indicate only one congregation in Philippi.

It is strange that people have little difficulty accepting a plurality of deacons, but are almost irrationally frightened by a plurality of overseers that is far more clearly demonstrated in the New Testament. The New Testament informs us that the pastoral oversight of many of the first churches was committed to a council of elders (overseers). This was true of the earliest Jewish congregations in Jerusalem (Acts 11:30; 15:6; 21:18), Judea, and neighboring countries (James 5:14), as well as in many of the first Gentile churches.

At the end of Paul's first missionary journey (southern area of Galatia), he and Barnabas traveled back through their newly planted congregations at Derbe, Lystra, Iconium, and Antioch and appointed a body of elders for each church: "And when they had appointed elders for them in every church [the Greek text says, "church by church, elders"], having prayed with fasting, they commended them to the Lord in whom they had believed" (Acts 14:23).

Near the end of his life, Paul directed Titus to appoint elders for churches on the island of Crete. He writes, "For this reason I left you in Crete, that you might set in order what remains, and appoint elders in every city as I directed you" (Titus 1:5). We also know that Paul established a body of elders in the churches of Ephesus and Philippi (Acts 20:17; 1 Timothy 5:17; Philippians 1:1), and most likely the church in Thessalonica (1 Thessalonians 5:12).

Writing to a whole string of churches in the northwestern part of Asia Minor (Pontus, Galatia, Cappadocia, Asia, and Bithynia), Peter urgently exhorts "the elders among you" to do the work of shepherding the flock of God" (1 Peter 5:1,2).

By the term "elders," Paul, Peter, James, and Luke refer to the elder-system of government, as amply witnessed by the Old Testament. (It is also displayed in all the churches of the second century. Each local church had a bishop, a council of elders, and a body of deacons.) This ancient system of government is corporate rule by the qualified, leading men of society, often called "elders."

7. At the beginning of the second century, many churches developed three separate offices or leadership ministries. That was the start of episcopally structured churches:

> The overseer (bishop)
> A council of elders
> A body of deacons

At the start of the second century, the bishop (overseer) presided over one local church, not a group of churches. Thus he is called the monarchical bishop. Progressively through the centuries, inordinate authority became concentrated in the bishop. Unchecked by New Testament Scriptures, his role continued to expand. The bishop became ruler over a group of churches. Some bishops emerged as supreme over other bishops. Eventually they formed councils of bishops. Finally in the West one bishop emerged as head over every Christian and every church.

But in the churches of the New Testament period, there was no clearly defined, three-office system. Instead, there were only two offices as found in Philippians 1:1.

> The council of overseer-elders
> The body of deacons

8. W.A. Jurgens, ed. and trans., *The Faith of the Early Fathers,* 3 vols. (Collegeville, MN: The Liturgical Press, 1979), 2:194.

NOTES

9. J.B. Lightfoot, *Saint Paul's Epistles to the Philippians,* (London: Macmillan and Co., 1894), p. 99.

10. Ibid, p. 95.

11. The noun *shepherd* or *pastor* is only used once to describe Christian leaders, and that is in the context of spiritual gifts (Ephesians 4:11). The verb *shepherd* is used three times in the context of Christian leaders. Our Lord ordered Peter to "shepherd My sheep" (John 21:16). The elders' duty is to shepherd the church, and twice they are reminded to shepherd the flock of God (Acts 20:28; 1 Peter 5:2).

    Only two offices are described in the New Testament: elder and deacon. There is no third office of shepherd (pastor). To avoid confusing the office with the spiritual gift, we can say that some elders will have the gift of pastoring (shepherding), but not all. In summary, the eldership is the official shepherding body of the local church, and some of the elders will have the spiritual gift of shepherding.

12. Nigel Turner, *Christian Words* (Nashville: Thomas Nelson Publishers, 1981), p. viii.

Chapter 6: Deacons

1. For examples of *diakonos* used as officers in secular sources, see Hermann W. Beyer, *"diakonos,"* in *Theological Dictionary of the New Testament,* 2 (1964):91,92. Also see F. J. A. Hort's quote from Aeschines' letter against Ctesiphon (*Against Ctesiphon* 13 & 15) in *The Christian Ecclesia,* (London: Macmillan and Company, 1914), p. 211.

2. C.E.B. Cranfield, "Diakonia in the New Testament," in *Service in Christ: Essays Presented to Karl Barth on his 80th Birthday,* ed. J.I. Mc Cord and T.H.L. Parker (Grand Rapids: William B. Eerdmans Publishing Company, 1966), p.39.

3. F.J.A. Hort, *The Christian Ecclesia,* p. 209.

4. In Romans 12:7*a* Paul speaks of the gift of "service" (*diakonian*). Some commentators think this gift refers to the office of deacon. Paul's focus in this passage, however, is on function and activity generally in the body, not specifically on church offices. It is highly unlikely that Paul is thinking exclusively of the office of deacon. Instead he is referring to all who would have the gift of service—some of course would be deacons.

    A Christian may have the gift of "service," or "giving" (Romans 12:8*b*), or "mercy" (Romans 12:8*d*), yet at the same time not desire or qualify to be a deacon. That person should still serve the body with the gift God has given (1 Peter 4:10). Of course each deacon would have his particular gift. So the gifts of "giving," "mercy," and "helps" would be found among the deacons. In 1 Corinthians 12:28 there is the gift of "helps" (Greek, *antilēmpsis*). It is certainly a gift some deacons should have. Yet it is doubtful that Paul means to refer exclusively to deacons by the word "helps." In his list of qualifications for deacons, Paul requires no special spiritual gift.

In any healthy, local church there must be many people working in various programs and at different levels that have the spiritual gifts—all in different measure—of "service," "teaching," "helps," and "leading," yet who are not overseers or deacons. Paul's lists of spiritual gifts allow for a great deal of flexibility and diversity.

5. Some scholars think that deacons were primarily personal assistants to the overseers. This view is very appealing, and there is some truth to it. But if New Testament deacons were assistants to overseers, that would probably have been made plain by the Greek term *hypēretēs,* meaning "assistants," not by *diakonoi.* Although the two words *diakonos* and *hypēretēs* are very similar, the latter stresses more the idea of "helper" or "assistant" in the official sense (Acts 13:5; Luke 4:20).

Furthermore, deacons are never described in the New Testament as "their [overseers] servants" or "their helpers." Finally, Acts 6 confirms that deacons form a complementary office to overseers, and that they are not merely assistant overseers.

6. The number of post-biblical statements about deacons' duties is sparse, often ambiguous, and sometimes conflicting, but here are some key examples of deacons serving the needy.

On his way to Rome, escorted by ten Roman soldiers to face martyrdom, Ignatius wrote seven letters (c. A.D. 115). In his letter to the church in Tralles, he writes:

And those likewise who are deacons of the mysteries of Jesus Christ must please all men in all ways. For they are not deacons of meats and drinks but servants of the Church of God. It is right therefore that they should beware of blame as of fire (*Trallians,* 2; Lightfoot, *Apostolic Fathers*).

From the brief phrase, "not deacons of meats and drinks," we may rightly assume that the deacons administered food to the needy. It appears that Polybius, the bishop of Tralles, informed Ignatius about certain complaints about the deacons— perhaps, conflict over their duties. So Ignatius gently reminds the deacons that they "must please all men in all ways" and "beware of blame as of fire." Note, too, that Ignatius tells them that they have been called to be "servants of the Church of God," not merely servants of food.

Shepherd of Hermas, the popular and visionary *Pilgrim's Progress* of the early centuries of Christianity, was written in Rome during the first half of the second century. Addressing the problem of evil deacons, Hermas writes:

> They that have the spots are deacons that exercised their office ill, and plundered the livelihood of widows and orphans, and made gain for themselves from the ministrations which they had received to perform (*Parables* 9.26; Lightfoot, *Apostolic Fathers*).

According to Hermas, deacons distribute alms and specifically care for widows and orphans. Thus those deacons who have misused their trust must repent and "fulfil their ministrations [*diakonian*] in purity" (*Parables* 9:26).

The apocalyptic book, *Vision of Paul* (c. A.D. 240, from Egypt), envisions deacons severely suffering in hell for stealing the people's offerings for the poor (*Ante-Nicene Fathers,* 10:160.).

Justin Martyr (c. A.D. 100-165), a converted pagan philosopher, was a prominent Christian apologist, writer, and teacher during the second century. In his book, *First Apology,* he provides a rare glimpse into a Christian church service in Rome about A.D. 150. In his description, he mentions that deacons distribute the bread and wine of the Lord's Supper to those present and then take the elements to those who are absent, most likely as a result of sickness or infirmity:

> And when the president has given thanks, and all the people have expressed their assent, those who are called by us deacons give to each of those present to partake of the bread and wine mixed with water over which the thanksgiving was pronounced, and to those who are absent they carry away a portion (*Ante-Nicene Fathers,* 1:185).

By the middle of the second century, the bishop was responsible to help the poor and administer the church's funds, as well as supervise every other area of church life. The deacon was the bishop's agent of information and administrator of poor relief.

"In primitive times," writes Anglican church historian, Edwin Hatch (1835-1889), "every case of poverty or suffering had been separately known to the bishop, and personally relieved by a deacon" (*The Organization of the Early Christian Churches* [London: Longmans, Green, and Company, 1901], p.50).

Hans Lietzmann (1875-1942), renowned church historian from the University of Berlin, tells us that Fabian, the bishop of Rome (A.D.236-250), divided Rome into seven districts and placed a deacon over each in order to administer care for the poor:

> In the metropolis of Rome, care for the poor was, by the nature of the case, a problem which the church found as important as it was difficult. It became such an essential duty of the deacons that, in the course of time, they were deprived of the liturgical functions which were regarded as obviously theirs in other districts. Whereas in other places the number of deacons might be increased at will according to the requirements of the church, it remained in Rome at the number seven sanctified by Acts 6:5.... Up to this period, the activity of the deacons had not been limited according to the quarters of the city, but Fabian divided the city into seven districts, setting a deacon over each (*The Founding of the Church Universal* [London: Lutterworth Press, 1938], p. 249-250).

The *Didascalia Apostolorum,* a church order manual (c. A.D. 230) representing the East in Syria, has much to say about deacons. Although deacons are the bishop's closest assistants and highly influential in the church, their practical servant position is still highlighted:

> If then our Lord did thus, will you, O deacons, hesitate to do the like for them that are sick and infirm, you who are work-men of the truth, and bear the likeness of Christ?... It is required of you deacons therefore that you visit all who are in need, and inform the bishop of those who are in distress..." (trans., R.H. Connolly [Oxford: Clarendon Press, 1929], p. 150).

The *Didascalia* also states:

> And in proportion to the number of the congregation of the people of the Church, so let the deacons be, that they may be able to take knowledge of (each) severally and refresh all; so

173

that for the aged women who are infirm, and for brethren and sisters who are in sickness—for every one they may provide the ministry which is proper for him (p. 148).

The *Epistle of Clement to James* states that deacons are to inform the bishop of the peoples' needs and sins, control disorderly people during church services, and report to the congregation on those who are sick and need help: "And let them learn who are suffering under bodily disease, and let them bring them to the notice of the multitude..." (*Ante-Nicene Fathers,* 8:220).

Although these post-biblical authors do not carry apostolic authority like Paul and Luke, and are often unbiblical in their own church practices regarding deacons, they demonstrate that a primary part of the deacons' duties was ministering to the people's practical, physical needs.

7. R. P. Symonds, "Deacons in the Early Church," *Theology* 58 (November, 1955): 408.

Chapter 7: The Absolute Necessity for Character Qualifications

1. Jerome, "Letters 52," in the *The Nicene and Post-Nicene Fathers,* 14 vols., Second Series, eds. Philip Schaff and Henry Wace (repr. Grand Rapids: William B. Eerdmans Publishing Company, n.d.) 6:94. (Hereafter cited as *The Nicene and Post-Nicene Fathers.*)
2. W. M. Ramsay quoted by Walter Lock in *The Pastoral Epistles,* The International Critical Commentary (Edinburgh: T.& T. Clark, 1924), p. 42.
3. Walter Bauer, *A Greek-English Lexicon of the New Testament and Other Early Christian Literature,* 2nd ed., trans. William F. Arndt and F. Wilbur Gingrich, rev. F. Wilbur Gingrich and Frederick W. Danker (Chicago: University of Chicago Press, 1979), p. 61.
4. E. F. Scott, *The Pastoral Epistles,* The Moffatt New Testament Commentary (London: Hodder and Stoughton, 1936), p. 38.
5. David C. Verner, *The Household of God: The Social World of the Pastoral Epistles,* SBL Dissertation Series, 71 (Chico, CA: Scholar Press, 1983), p. 110.
6. J.N.D. Kelly, *The Pastoral Epistles* (London: Adam and Charles Black, 1972), p. 86.
7. Francis A. Schaeffer, *The Church at the End of the 20th Century* (Downers Grove: InterVarsity Press, 1970), p. 65.

8. In Philippians 1:1 and Acts 20:28 the term *overseers* is in the plural form, but in Timothy 3:2 and Titus 1:7 we find *overseer* in the singular form. There is no discrepancy in these differences, however. In 1 Timothy 3 and Titus 1, Paul uses a generic or generalizing singular. That means the one overseer represents the entire group of overseers and all that should be characteristic of that group. Thus, *overseer* stands for all overseers.

In the same way, in 1 Timothy 5:3,5,9 Paul uses the generic singular *widow* for widows, he certainly doesn't mean that only one widow was in the church or that only one widow can be put on a widow's list for financial help. It is obvious he is using a generic singular. Therefore, no convincing argument can be made for the second century practice of elevating one man—the overseer/bishop—over the elders, deacons, and congregation, based on the singular use of overseer in 1 Timothy 3:2.

9. James M. Boice, *Foundations of the Christian Faith* (Downers Grove: InterVarsity Press, 1986), p. 632.

Chapter 8: Five Character Qualifications for Deacons

1. Richard C. Trench, *Synonyms of the New Testament* (1880; repr. Grand Rapids: William B. Eerdmans Publishing Company, 1969), p. 348.
2. Richard Belward Rackham, *The Acts of the Apostles,* Westminster Commentaries (London: Methuen and Company, 1901), p. 83.
3. John Calvin, *Acts,* 1:162.
4. J.N.D. Kelly, *The Pastoral Epistles* (London: Adam and Charles Black, 1972), p. 81.
5. Lawrence O. Richards, *Expository Dictionary of Bible Words* (Grand Rapids: Zondervan Publishing House, 1985), p. 187.
6. George W. Knight, III, *The Pastoral Epistles, A Commentary on the Greek Text,* The New International Greek Testament Commentary (Grand Rapids: William B. Eerdmans Publishing Company, 1992), p.169.
7. J.N.D. Kelly, *The Pastoral Epistles,* p. 47.
8. W. E. Vine, *An Expository Dictionary of New Testament Words* 4 vols. (Kansas City: Walterick Publishers, 1969), 3:51.
9. The definite article suggests that "the faith" refers to the objective truths or doctrines of Christianity. (See also 1 Timothy 4:1,6; 5:8; 6:10; 2 Timothy 3:8.)
10. Homer Kent, *The Pastoral Epistles,* (Chicago: Moody Press, 1958), p. 139.

Chapter 9: Qualification Demands Examination

1. Some commentators deny that the "and...also" (Greek, *kai...de*) construction refers back to overseers. They contend that these words only add a further precaution about deacons. For example, Alford writes, "the *de* introduces a caution—the slight contrast of a necessary addition to their mere present character" (Henry Alford, *The Greek New Testament*, 4 vols. [5th ed., London: Rivingtons, 1871], 3:327.)

   It is difficult to be certain, but the Greek construction, *kai* ("also") before *houtoi* ("these"), seems best served by understanding that deacons are compared with overseers in the testing process. It creates no problem, however, if the text does not refer back to the overseers. 1 Timothy 5:24,25 shows that an examination of elders was necessary, and by inference if overseers needed to be examined as to their qualifications, so do deacons. As long as character qualifications are demanded, examination will also be demanded.

2. Richard C. Trench, *Synonyms of the New Testament* (1880; repr. Grand Rapids: William B. Eerdmans Publishing Company, 1969), p. 278.

3. Walter Grundmann, *"dokimazō,"* in *Theological Dictionary of the New Testament*, 2:256. Hermann Cremer, *"dokimazō,"* in *Biblico-Theological Lexicon of New Testament Greek,* trans., W. Urwick, (1895; repr. Greenwood, SC: The Attic Press, Inc., 1977), pp. 699,700.

4. Walter Bauer, *A Greek-English Lexicon of the New Testament and Other Early Christian Literature*, 2nd ed., trans. William F. Arndt and F. Wilbur Gingrich, rev. F. Wilbur Gingrich and Frederick W. Danker (Chicago: The University of Chicago Press, 1979), p. 202.

5. F.F. Bruce, *The Letters of Paul* (Grand Rapids: William E. Eerdmans Publishing Company, 1965), p. 307.

6. See my chapter, "The Laying on of Hands and Ordination," in *Biblical Eldership: An Urgent Call To Restore Biblical Church Leadership* (Littleton, CO: Lewis and Roth Publishers, 1988), pp. 223-237.

Chapter 10: Qualifications for Wives Who Assist Their Deacon Husbands

1. For a thorough defense of the historical, Christian position of male headship and female subordination, see the excellent volume edited by John Piper and Wayne Grudem entitled

Recovering Biblical Manhood and Womanhood (Wheaton: Crossway Books, 1991).

2. Patrick Fairbairn, *Pastoral Epistles* (1874; repr. Minneapolis, MN: James and Klock Publishing Company, 1976), p.150.

3. Phoebe was an outstanding Christian woman (Romans 16:1,2). Paul speaks of her as a "helper of many, and of myself as well." Some commentators conjecture that Phoebe was a wealthy and influential patroness of the Lord's work at Cenchrea. Whatever help she supplied, in a unique way she was a distinguished servant of the church. In all probability, Paul is commending her for extraordinary service by means of this beautiful description, "servant of the church." Paul and Luke customarily describe others by their work or faithfulness, not by official titles. If Paul is calling Phoebe a "deacon of the church," it would be a unique exception to his usual practice.

The example of Phoebe illustrates the preeminent service that Christian women provided for the Lord's work during New Testament times. Because women are not to be officers in the church doesn't mean that they can't significantly serve the church or their Lord. Every Christian woman should wholeheartedly serve the body of Christ. Let us not forget that humble, self-sacrificing service to others, not position or status, is the supreme mark of greatness in God's eyes (Mark 9:33-37; 10:35-45).

Some scholars think that there is a reference to women deacons in Pliny's letter to Emperor Trajan that is dated c. A.D. 112. Seeking more accurate information about Christians, Pliny the Younger, governor of Bithynia, tells Emperor Trajan that he tortured two Christian women who were called *ministrae* (Latin for "servants"). In a section of the letter reporting the confessions of people who once professed Christianity but turned away, Pliny writes,

> I judged it so much the more necessary to extract the real truth, with the assistance of torture, from two female slaves [*ancillae,* "handmaids"], who were styled *deaconesses* [*ministrae,* "servants"]: but I could discover nothing more than depraved and excessive superstition (*Pliny,* 2 vols., trans., W. Melmoth Trajan, The Loeb Classical Library [Cambridge: Harvard University Press, 1961], 2:405).

The problem with the reference to *ministrae* (servants) is ambiguity, the same as in Romans 16:1. The translators have rendered the Latin *ministrae* as "deaconesses," but "servants" is

177

an equally valid translation. There is no way of knowing if these women were official deacons or not.

4. I am indebted to Gordon H. Clark for this idea. See Gordon H. Clark, *The Pastoral Epistles* (Jefferson, MD: The Trinity Foundation, 1983), p.61.

5. For an outstanding description of biblical manhood and womanhood, read John Piper, "A Vision of Biblical Complementarity: Manhood and Womanhood Defined According to the Bible" in *Recovering Biblical Manhood and Womanhood*, pp. 31-59.

6. It is remarkable that deaconesses are not mentioned in the letters of Ignatius (c. A.D. 115), although he was nearly obsessed with speaking of church offices. Deaconesses also do not appear in Polycarp's letter to Philippi or in the writings of Tertullian (North Africa). In the well-known church order manual, *Apostolic Tradition* (c. A.D. 220), which was written from Rome by Hippolytus, all the various categories of ministries of the church in Rome are listed. Hippolytus speaks of bishops, priests, deacons, subdeacons, confessors, widows, lectors, virgins, healers, but not of deaconesses.

The first uncontested, concrete information on women deacons is found in the *Didascalia Apostolorum* ("Teaching of the Apostles"). The *Didascalia* is a church order manual. It is dated around A.D. 230 and was composed in northern Syria by an unknown bishop. It thus represents eastern Christianity.

The *Didascalia* teaches that women deacons are to visit Christian women who are ill, but live in pagan households where Christian men cannot visit. They also are to help the bishop in the baptism of women by anointing the women candidates with oil before baptism. Following baptism, they are to instruct the newly baptized women concerning holy living. The female deacon, however, was not to baptize as the bishop, presbyters, or male deacons could: "...whether thou [bishop] thyself baptize, or thou command the deacons or presbyters to baptize—let a woman deacon, as we have already said, anoint the women. But let a man pronounce over them the invocation of the divine Names in the water" (*Didascalia Apostolorum* trans. R. Hugh Connolly [Oxford: Clarendon Press, 1929], pp. 145,146.

Concerning the differences between deacons and deaconesses in the *Didascalia,* Aime Georges Martimort concludes:

The roles were thus not exactly parallel. Deaconesses took no part in the liturgy. Indeed, their part in the rite of baptism itself was very restricted; they simply completed the anointing begun by the celebrant. Nor did they pronounce the invocation, or epiclesis. In no way could they be considered on the same level as deacons: they were their auxiliaries (*Deaconesses: An Historical Study* [San Francisco: Ignatius Press, 1986], p.43.).

The largest church order book is *Apostolic Constitutions,* dated around A.D. 380. The author appears to be an eastern Arian Christian. *Apostolic Constitutions* provides a good deal of information on deaconesses. (The following references are taken from *Apostolic Constitutions* [also called *Constitutions of the Holy Apostles*] in volume 7 of *The Ante-Nicene Fathers.*)

The deaconess distributes charity to the poor and widows (7:430). She keeps the door by which the women enter the church and supervises their behavior during worship (7:421). She is the liaison between the women of the church and the clergy. In broad terms, she is responsible for the care of the women of the church: "And let the deaconess be diligent in taking care of the women" (7:432). According to the *Constitutions,* the deaconess was ordained and a member of the lower clergy (7:492). She was also to be "a pure virgin; or, at the least, a widow who has been but once married, faithful, and well esteemed" (7:457).

Although there are close parallels between the deacon and deaconess in *Apostolic Constitutions,* the office of deaconess is not identical to the male diaconate. In the ordination prayer for the deaconess said by the bishop, nothing is said of higher office, but for the deacon it is stated, "Do thou render him worthy to discharge acceptably the ministration of a deacon...that thereby he may attain an higher degree..." (7:492). More to the point, *Apostolic Constitutions* states:

> But it is not lawful for any one of the other clergy to do the work of a deacon. A deaconess does not bless, nor perform anything belonging to the office of presbyters or deacons, but only is to keep the doors, and to minister to the presbyters in the baptizing of women, on account of decency. A deacon separates [chooses or dedicates] a sub-deacon, a reader, a singer, and a deaconess, if there be any occasion, in the absence of a presbyter. It is not lawful for a sub-deacon to separate either one of the clergy or laity; nor for a reader, nor for a singer, nor for a deaconess, for they are the ministers to the deacons (7:494).

7. Roger Gryson, *The Ministry of Women in the Early Church*, trans. Jean Laporte and Mary Louise Hall (Collegeville, MN: The Liturgical Press, 1976), p.15.

8. Aime George Martimort, *Deaconesses: An Historical Study*, trans. K.D. Whitehead (San Francisco: Ignatius Press, 1982), p.247.

   In his judicious work, *The Office of Woman in the Church*, Fritz Zerbst, a German Lutheran theologian, comments: "Even in its highest development the office of deaconess never achieved more than the right to render modest auxiliary services at baptisms and to instruct female candidates for baptism" (*The Office of Woman in the Church* [St. Louis: Concordia Publishing House, 1955] p. 91).

9. William Hendriksen, *Exposition of the Pastoral Epistles*, New Testament Commentary (Grand Rapids: Baker Book House, 1957) p. 133.

10. George W. Knight, III, *Commentary on 1 Timothy*, New International Greek Testament Commentary (Grand Rapids: William B. Eerdmans Publishing Company, 1992), p.172.

11. A few well-known biblical commentators believe that these are the wives of both overseers and deacons. This is unlikely. The words in verse 11, "wives likewise must be dignified," parallels exactly what is said about deacons in verse 8, "deacons likewise must be dignified." Also, the qualifications for the wives nearly parallel those of the deacons (verses 8,9). Finally, the position of this instruction on wives, wedged in the middle of instruction on deacons, convinces most interpreters that if wives are mentioned here, then they are the wives of the deacons, to whom they are made parallel.

12. Luke 1:25,30,36-38,41-55,60; 2:19,34,35,51; 7:36-50; 8:3,48; 10:38-42; 13:12-16; 18:3-6; 21:2; 23:27,55,56; 24:1-11, 22,23; Acts 1:14; 2:17,18; 8:12; 16:14,15,40.

13. The Greek word *nēphalios* means "wineless" or sobriety in the use of wine. A few interpreters think the word should be understood here in its literal sense, but that is doubtful. In 1 Timothy 3:2 Paul uses *nēphalios* as a qualification for overseers. Then in verse 3, he writes that overseers must not be "addicted to wine." Paul is not warning overseers twice about the use of wine. Instead, he is using the word "temperate," both in verse 2 and here in verse 11, figuratively to mean mental and emotional sobriety.

14. Lawrence O. Richards, *Expository Dictionary of Biblical Words* (Grand Rapids: Zondervan Publishing House, 1985), p. 260.

Chapter 11: Family Requirements for Deacons

1. Many Bible teachers believe that "the sons of God" are fallen angels (Job 1:6; 2:1; Daniel 3:25; 1Peter 3:19,20; Jude 6), not the sons of Seth. Admittedly this is a difficult passage, but on the whole I favor the view that refers "sons of God" to the godly line of Seth (Genesis 4:26; 5:3ff.; Deuteronomy 14:1). See H.C. Leupold, *Exposition of Genesis,* 2 vols. (Grand Rapids: Baker Book House, 1942), 1:249-254. John Murray, *Principles of Conduct* (Grand Rapids: William B. Eerdmans Publishing Company, 1957), pp.243-249.

   For an excellent treatment of 1 Peter 3:19,20 see Wayne Grudem, *1 Peter,* Tyndale New Testament Commentaries (Grand Rapids: William B. Eerdmans Publishing Company, 1990), pp.203- 239.

2. D. Martyn Lloyd-Jones, *Studies in the Sermon on the Mount* 2 vols. (Grand Rapids: William B. Eerdmans Publishing Company, 1971), 1:37.

3. Some people teach that the phrase "the husband of one wife" means married only once in a lifetime. Although this view seems to have the literalness of the phrase in its favor, and so must be taken seriously, it is in disharmony with the overall biblical teaching regarding marriage for several reasons. Here is why:

   (1) The Bible unequivocally teaches that death dissolves the marriage bond and frees the living spouse to remarry without sinning (1 Corinthians 7:39; Romans 7:2,3).

   (2) From the biblical perspective, remarriage after the death of a spouse is not reproachful. Those who hold the married-only-once view cannot identify the shame or defect in remarriage that disqualifies a man from eldership or deaconship. This is especially true of deacons. Since deacons are not the spiritual overseers of the church, it is close to impossible to understand the reproach deacons would face if remarried after the death of a spouse. In fact, *those who try to show the reproach of a second marriage only raise serious questions about the first marriage as well.*

   This interpretation smacks of false asceticism, the very thing Paul condemns in 1 Timothy 4:3. Of the false teachers at Ephesus, Paul says they are "men who forbid marriage and advocate abstaining from foods...." Yet this interpretation makes Paul forbid a second marriage to church leaders and needy widows.

(3) This interpretation creates two standards for two grades of saints. For some bewildering reason, elders, deacons, and needy widows cannot remarry following the death of a spouse, but other saints can. Such division in the family of God is incongruous with the rest of the New Testament. "To postulate grades of official sanctity," E.K. Simpson writes, "among members of the same spiritual body may be orthodox clericalism, but it is heterodox Christianity" (*The Pastoral Epistles* [Grand Rapids: William B. Eerdmans Publishing Company, 1954], p.50).

(4) In the context of instruction on marriage, singleness, and remarriage, Paul says to the Corinthians, "And this I say for your own benefit; not to put a restraint upon you . . ." (1 Corinthians 7:35). This interpretation, however, restrains an innocent man, penalizing him for not having the gift of singleness.

(5) First Timothy 5:9 lists the qualifications for widows who the local church is obligated to support: "Let a widow be put on the list only if she is not less than sixty years old, having been the wife of one man...." If the phrase "the wife of one man" means only one husband in a lifetime, then Paul's counsel five verses later to younger widows to remarry is very confusing. In verse 14 Paul urges younger widows to marry: "Therefore, I want younger widows to get married, bear children, keep house, and give the enemy no occasion for reproach." What if a widow's second husband were to die? Would she then no longer be eligible for the widows' roll because she followed the apostle's advice to remarry when she was young? This would be confusing counsel indeed. Of course if the phrase "the wife of one man" doesn't mean one husband in a lifetime then there is no conflict in Paul's counsel.

(6) It is almost unthinkable that Paul, who is so sensitive to marital issues (1 Corinthians 7:2-5,7,8,15,32-36,39), would use an ambiguous three-word phrase to teach something so vital to widows and widowers that is in apparent disharmony with the rest of Scripture. In 1 Corinthians, where Paul counsels unmarried Christians to consider singleness, he is quick to qualify his words. He knew the propensity to asceticism. He knew that people could take his words to mean he was speaking disparagingly of marriage. But in no way is he discrediting marriage.

Marriage is the norm, but singleness, which Paul wants us to consider, can be effectively used to further the work of God. So he writes, "Yet I wish that all men were even as I myself am. However, each man has his own gift from God, one in this manner, and another in that. But I say to the unmarried and to widows that it is good for them if they remain even as I. But if they do not have self-control, let them marry, for it is better to marry than to burn" (1 Corinthians 7:7-9). This counsel is for elders and deacons, as well as for every other member of the congregation. If a deacon is a widower and decides to remain single for greater undivided service to God, that is good. But if he must marry, that is also acceptable.

(7) Finally, if this phrase means married only once, it is an extremely frightening and potentially harmful restriction. In the age that Paul wrote, and for the next eighteen hundred years, it was not uncommon for a person to lose a spouse through death at a relatively early age. So if a good elder or deacon lost his wife and remarried, he also lost his place of leadership in the church. That hurts the whole church. We all know good elders and deacons are hard to find. So to disqualify an elder or deacon because he remarried is a terrible loss. We know that God loves the church. Thus it is hard to believe that He would place a requirement upon its leaders that would hurt them or the church.

4. J.E. Huther, *Critical and Exegetical Hand-book to the Epistles to Timothy and Titus,* Meyer's Commentary on the New Testament (New York: Funk and Wagnalls, 1890), p. 118.
5. Elton Trueblood, *Your Other Vocation* (New York: Harper and Row, 1952), p. 82.

Chapter 12: The Significance and Rewards of Deacons

1. J. E. Huther, *Critical and Exegetical Handbook to the Epistles to Timothy and Titus,* Meyer's Commentary on the New Testament (New York: Funk and Wagnalls, 1890), p. 125.
2. E. K. Simpson, *The Pastoral Epistles* (Grand Rapids: William B. Eerdmans Company, 1954), p.57.
3. F.J.A. Hort, *The Christian Ecclesia,* (London: Macmillan and Company, 1914), p. 202.
4. Nigel Turner, *Christian Words* (Nashville: Thomas Nelson Publishers, 1981), p. 158.

5. Os Guinness, *In Two Minds: the dilemma of doubt and how to resolve it,* (Downers Grove: InterVarsity Press, 1976), pp. 49,150.

Chapter 13: Agents of Christ's Mercy

1. Lawrence O. Richards, *Expository Dictionary of Bible Words* (Grand Rapids: Zondervan Publishing House, 1985), p. 441.
2. C. E. Armerding, "Mercy, Merciful," in *The Zondervan Pictorial Encyclopedia of the Bible,* ed. M. C. Tenney, 5 vols. (Grand Rapids: Zondervan Publishing House, 1975), 4:188.
3. Timothy J. Keller, *Ministries of Mercy* (Grand Rapids: Zondervan Publishing House, 1989), p. 46.
4. Ibid., p. 46.

SCRIPTURE INDEX

SCRIPTURE INDEX

SCRIPTURE INDEX

SCRIPTURE INDEX

GENERAL INDEX

A GUIDE TO MORE EFFECTIVE ELDERS' MEETINGS

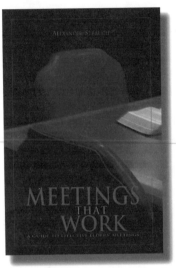

Meetings That Work:
A Guide to Effective Elders' Meetings

Are your elders' meetings satisfying and productive, or do they drag on with little accomplished? Does your group spend too much time on trivial matters? Do you find it hard to stay on track when discussing important issues?

If you are less than satisfied with the quality of your meetings, you are not alone. These are just a few of the common complaints. The fact is, good meetings don't just happen. People have to learn how to lead and how to participate in meetings effectively.

This book is designed to help you do just that. It describes, step by step, how to implement changes that can significantly improve your elders' meetings. It provides insightful information that every participant needs to know.

Although it is written primarily for church elders, *Meetings That Work* can be readily adapted by deacons or any church committee to improve the quality of their meetings.

Part 1 gives a fresh perspective on the significance of elders meetings. Part 2, the heart of the book, explains specifically how to go about improving your meetings. It covers biblical ground rules of conduct, personal participation, communication tools, facilitation, and the specifics of good meeting management. Part 3 includes questions and assignments that will help your group evaluate its strengths and weaknesses and identify areas for improvement. It outlines a step-by-step plan for discussing and implementing the suggestions in this book.